LENIN
STALIN
KHRUSHCHEV

LENIN
STALIN
KHRUSHCHEV
VOICES OF BOLSHEVISM

Edited by

Robert H. McNeal

A SPECTRUM BOOK

PRENTICE-HALL, INC.
Englewood Cliffs, N.J.

To Martha, Andrew, and Jeffrey

CONTENTS

STALIN

KHRUSHCHEV

LENIN
STALIN
KHRUSHCHEV

INTRODUCTION

Russian Communism (or Bolshevism) has been consistently concerned with the problem of power—its acquisition and maintenance—and this, in a general way, is the theme of the present anthology. This is not to assume that Lenin and his heirs have been wholly cynical concerning the moral justification of the power that they sought and gained; I doubt that this is true even of Stalin and Khrushchev. But the power to determine the "truth" and to direct a sizable part of humanity has been assumed by the Bolshevik leaders as the prerequisite to any humanitarian achievement. To the outsider, Bolshevik theory and practice may at times seem antithetical, but from within the system they are harmonized by their common assumption that the movement is nothing without power.

Bolshevik concern for the acquisition and maintenance of almost unlimited power has quite naturally led to a tradition of personal dictatorship; thus, in a short introduction to the cardinal writings of Bolshevism, there is something to be gained by restricting the collection to the works of Lenin, Stalin, and Khrushchev. Although there are many documents of great importance in the history of the Communist Party of the Soviet Union which are not the personal work of these rulers, the individual dictator embodies the principle of concentrated authority in theory and in practice—and these three successive dictators provide a continuous assertion of this principle. As much as the personal style of the three varies and as changeable as the particular issues of the day may be, there is a thread of tradition from Lenin's "What Is to Be Done?" (1902) to Khrushchev's critique of the "antiparty group" in 1961.

To be sure, this thread is tied to another thread running back to Marx and Engels; so one may object that the present anthology does not include any of their works or any of the expositions of their general ideas by Lenin or his successors. Marxism does form the background of Bolshevism and to some extent it dictates the limits of its flexibility in theory and practice, but the point here is that fundamental Marxism is not admitted to be an issue in Bolshevism. Instead, it is assumed to be the correct way of thinking and not subject to any doubt or question, whereas the important issues of Bolshevism that do require argumentation are distinct from Marxism in general. For example, Lenin, Stalin, or Khrushchev usually do not feel any need to dwell on materialism or surplus value and are much more concerned with such problems as the need to eliminate factions within Bolshevism or with the problem of the timing of the proletarian revolution in, say, Germany, taking for granted the inevitability of such a revolution sooner or later. In short, such works as "The Communist Manifesto" or Stalin's "Dialectical and Historical Materialism" will not be found here. The reader who is not previously familiar with the general background of Marxism would, therefore, do well to find one of the numerous introductions to the subject.*

Within the Lenin-Stalin-Khrushchev continuum there are, of course, important variations. The very changes in literary form are manifestations of the evolving character of the Bolshevik movement. Lenin was a prolific pamphleteer throughout his career, as evidenced by such writings as "What Is to Be Done?" and "The Proletarian Revolution and the Renegade Kautsky." He also was a quasi-scholarly theoretician; his weighty books *The Development of Capitalism in Russia* and *Materialism and Empiriocriticism* do not fit into an anthology such as this one very well, but his booklets *Imperialism* and *State and Revolution*, excerpted below, reveal Lenin the serious intellectual. There is also Lenin the public administrator, delivering a kind of state-of-the-union address to the Supreme Soviet (see his comments on electrification in this anthology). But even here the intellectual, professorial tone—he even assigns reading to his listeners—breaks through the official, bureaucratic character of the speech.

The decline of pamphleteering after the death of Lenin is symptomatic of the waning of the old radical intelligentsia. The traditional pamphlet is a medium appropriate to men accustomed to open debate (even if, like Lenin, they aim to constrict it) and even at its most vulgar the authentic political pamphlet retains an intellectual aspiration that is absent in the more or less ghostwritten official report. It is this form of expression, saturated with a sense of vested interest, that best typifies Stalin (see his report on the Draft Constitution) and, even more, Khrushchev. True, Stalin attempted to maintain at least a pretense of Marxist scholarship in such quotation-ridden essays as "Foundations of Leninism" † and in his pedantic published replies to comrades' questions, as in the collage entitled "Economic Problems of Socialism in the USSR." Khrushchev, however, has not even done this, communicating torrentially through impromptu and prepared speeches (including so-called interviews) but almost never in any work that is primarily written rather than spoken (his article "On Peaceful Coexistence" is a very rare exception). Even Khru-

---

* A good, concise primer is R. N. Carew Hunt's *The Theory and Practice of Communism: An Introduction* (New York: The Macmillan Company, 1951). A good selection of primary materials is Karl Marx and Friedrich Engels, *Basic Writings on Politics and Philosophy*, ed. Lewis S. Feuer (New York: Doubleday & Co., Inc., Anchor Books, 1959).

† I have tried to spare the reader passages in which Lenin quotes at length from Marx and Engels or in which Stalin quotes at length from Lenin. Such passages may be useful to convey the exegetical spirit of Bolshevik scholarship, but they would in this instance amount to a rather unwieldly anthology within an anthology.

shchev's pretensions as a theoretician have not impelled him to take up the intellectually painful process of writing.

The shift in form and style is not without major significance, representing the transition from the party led by intelligentsia, ascetic and ready to storm the gates of heaven, to the party of tough administrators, conscious that they run the largest enterprise in the world. Understandably this has engendered some measure of conservatism. The imminent withering away of the state or the conflagration of proletarian revolution in the West have not been predicted by Stalin and Khrushchev as they were by Lenin. And Khrushchev's picture of the ultimate utopia is notably restrained when it comes to determining the "needs," according to which men will receive their share of material abundance. But the changes in style from Leninism to Khrushchevism should not blind the reader to the continuity of the essential. The lack of intellectual sophistication in Stalin led Trotsky to misjudge Stalin's capacity for Bolshevik leadership and, even after this error cost Trotsky his membership in the party, he inveighed against the "thermidorean" betrayal of Lenin by Stalin. Persuaded by Trotsky's eloquence and Stalin's bureaucratic style, many others have exaggerated the change and underrated the continuity in Bolshevism.

The party has adjusted itself—and in much more than literary style—to the major changes in its life over sixty years, but it is more accurate to regard this as the evolution of a continuous tradition than as a "retreat," "betrayal," or "thermidorean reaction." Documentary evidence such as the writings in this collection are one form of witness to this continuity. Monotonous reaffirmation of faith in the unity of the party, the Bolshevik monopoly on truth, the depravity of factionalism, the decadence of imperialism, and the radiance of eventual communist society is not equivalent to the betrayal of Bolshevik faith. It is true that it would be hard for any contemporary Bolshevik to make any theoretical "discovery" of the same fundamental importance as Lenin's theory of the monolithic party or of imperialism. But tedious repetition of old formulae has not so inhibited the imagination of present-day Bolsheviks that they are unable to adapt the old credos to such new problems as the nuclear threat.

Lenin is much more richly documented than his successors. Not only was he a far more versatile and prolific writer than Stalin and Khrushchev, he is also much less "classified." From Lenin's pen we have not only a bountiful supply of writings that he intended for publication but also many letters, first drafts, research notes, memoranda, and even a confidential testament. Even with Khrushchev's revelations about Stalin, we have no such store of writing from the hand of that dictator, who carefully chose what he wanted to have published and added very little indeed to his literary corpus after the Thirties.* One can only speculate concerning

---

* The main posthumous addition to our fund of Stalin material is the collection of his correspondence with the British and American heads of state during the wartime collaboration. It is important in its own way but reveals rather little about

the content of Stalin's official intra-Communist correspondence (excepting a few snippets) or his speeches to various high councils. Khrushchev is more prolific by far, and since 1953 has almost certainly outstripped even Lenin when it comes to average monthly verbiage in print. But, as noted earlier, this is almost solely restricted to published oratory. Not only is correspondence lacking but the oratory is carefully selected; we do not have any good account of the content of Khrushchev's speech against Molotov, Malenkov, *et al.* in the June, 1957, meeting of the Central Committee, which may well have been the most crucial of all his addresses.

A very large part of the writings of Lenin, Stalin, and Khrushchev (almost all the works of the last two) may be considered propaganda in the very broad sense that the various works were intended for publication with the definite intention of convincing somebody of something. For this reason it may be objected that a collection of the present sort is simply a mélange of deliberate falsification not worth reading. In reply, it may be said first that falsification (and sincere misunderstanding, too) is not a Bolshevik monopoly and, secondly, that all documents, especially those connected with a religious, social, or political movement, must be subjected to critical scrutiny. The introductory comments to each selection in this anthology are intended to sketch such elements of the background and to raise such issues as may assist the reader in maintaining a properly critical approach.

Moreover, the propagandistic intent of these writings does not preclude their having great value as sincere statements of fundamental belief. The most important writings are usually directed to the faithful followers of communism, not to unconverted outsiders, and in these cases sincere self-deception generally prevails over conscious falsification. For example, it is quite plausible to suppose that Lenin, Stalin, and Khrushchev have believed in the sanctity of party unity under their personal command and to suppose that their reiterated appeals for monolithic solidarity reflect not purely cynical self-aggrandizement but a sincere identification of their personal careers with the success of the movement. Even in those instances in which it is almost certain that the Bolshevik writer knew that he lied (as in Stalin's most exaggerated attacks on Trotsky), it is likely that he condoned his license by invoking the higher interest of the masses. And in the study of a movement based on dogma, it is at all times necessary to know what the leading "truths" may be, regardless of their objective validity or falsity. The dogma of the day may be propaganda, but very often it is, at the same time, a kind of tactical order or a reflection of some important development in intraparty affairs. Khrushchev's polemic against the antiparty group in 1961 is as propagandistic as any writing in the

Russian communism. See *Correspondence between the Chairman of the Council of Ministers of the U.S.S.R. and the Presidents of the U.S.A. and the Prime Ministers of Great Britain during the Great Patriotic War of 1941-1945* (2 vols., Moscow, 1957).

world, but it is also our best primary source on the major intraparty issues of the period.

The selection of material for this book has been partly shaped by the design of its companion volume, *The Bolshevik Tradition: Lenin, Stalin, Khrushchev.* The source documents that follow are intended to illuminate and buttress the *The Bolshevik Tradition*; but I hope that the selection is not concocted to suppress material that runs counter to my presentation in the companion volume. As much as I should like to attract the reader of these source documents to the accompanying book of interpretation, the two are intended to be useful as separate volumes; moreover, I have tried to select documents that would be recognized by most scholars in the field as major works.

This may raise the question, "Why bother with a new anthology?" There is a vast body of writing by Lenin which is available in English in pamphlet, selective collection, and, lately, complete works. The essentials of Stalin have, for years, been largely contained in the collection *Problems of Leninism,* supplemented by pamphlets, shorter anthologies, and the incomplete *Works* in English. Khrushchev is less reprinted than his predecessors, but English translations of most of his speeches are not hard to find in Soviet or western editions. Despite the existence of these works, convenience is an obvious and major justification for the present anthology. The source materials for this anthology are not buried in manuscript or in linguistic inaccessibility, but they are not easy to come by in compact form either. If Stalin had been left on his pedestal, we might have a Soviet version of an anthology of Lenin, Stalin, and Khrushchev but this is hardly likely while Stalin's bones remain so unhallowed. Even if a Soviet anthology of the three dictators' work did appear, political considerations would preclude the inclusion of documents that reveal the topsy-turvy fate of particular points, even though basic Bolshevik premises have survived all vicissitudes. Khrushchev's speeches of March, 1937, and February, 1956, both concerning the purges, are unlikely to appear together in any Soviet anthology (unless Khrushchev's successor throws Khrushchev's bones into potter's field). Finally, there is something to be said for annotation by a compiler who is not duty-bound to regard Lenin as infallible nor Trotsky as a renegade.

Stalin's writings pose a special problem. They span about fifty years, and roughly one-third of the volume of this material was written before Lenin died in 1924, which is before Stalin's writings were generally considered to be major documents of Bolshevism.* There is comparatively

* A few works on the question of nationality, especially the essay usually entitled "Marxism and the National Question," form an exception; the essay cited was reprinted twice before Lenin died. But a representative selection of writings by Lenin, Stalin, and Khrushchev on the question of nationality would require many pages. I have

little need to draw upon this portion of the available resources; so in the interests of concision I have not done so. This is not to imply that Stalin was of no account before 1924. It is true that he was not very well-known when Lenin died, but he already held more important offices in the Bolshevik-Soviet structure than any other individual. The point is rather that Stalin's usual strategy before Lenin died was to stick very close to Lenin on most issues, avoiding the fiery disputes that embroiled such colleagues as Trotsky, Zinoviev, Kamenev, and Bukharin. This modesty helped to delude other Bolsheviks concerning Stalin's real importance in the party and it also tended to prevent the publication by Stalin of works that add much to the mainstream of Bolshevism before 1924. On the first twenty years or more of Stalin's career we have a comparatively good supply of written material but rather little incentive to reprint it.

The situation is reversed in roughly the last twenty years of Stalin's career, when he was *the* Bolshevik, the sacred font of Leninist truth as well as the wielder of all instruments of physical power. It is really essential to include some idea of Stalin's views on a variety of major issues during these years, but the paucity of his published writing is such that one really can find nothing worth including on so important a subject as the emergent Communist bloc in East Europe and Asia. Even if the compilation made free use of documents from the Forties and early Fifties which are certainly not Stalin's personal work, it would be impossible to find published material to do justice to the period. Although Stalin's lieutenant A. A. Zhdanov did deliver some rather original pronouncements, presumably representing Stalin's wishes, the prevailing rule under mature Stalinism was that nobody publicly discussed a subject if the Leader had not pronounced on it and, after he had spoken, further discussion consisted only of echoes. For this reason there is rather little to be gained by attempting to supplement Stalin's own meager statements with those of his lieutenants or publicists. By the same token, there is little reason to include Khrushchev's writings from the Stalin era. However, the contrast between Khrushchev writing as a Stalinist in 1937 and as an anti-Stalinist in 1956 is too good to omit.

A few comments on matters of form complete this introduction. Existing translations have been used where convenient and the handiwork of the various translators has been untouched in the main. However, for the sake of technical uniformity, an attempt has been made to standardize matters of spelling and punctuation. All italicized emphasis is taken from the original edition, as are sub-headings within the excerpts. Footnotes have been added by the compiler.

---

regretfully concluded that it is better to omit the question of nationality (not to mention such questions as religion, military doctrine, and artistic criticism) in the interests of presenting a concise collection focused on issues of general importance.

LENIN

WHAT IS TO BE DONE?

In 1902 when Lenin published this pamphlet, Russia had known about seventy-five years of intermittent revolutionary spasms and about ten years of small-scale Marxist activity, but for all practical purposes there was still no "Social Democratic" (Marxist) Party in Russia, unlike most major European countries. It was to this immediate problem that Lenin's question, "What Is to Be Done?" was directed. How does one go about establishing a party? What sort of a party should it be?

When Lenin undertook this essay he was already over thirty and had written a number of Marxist works, notably a weighty economic study entitled *The Development of Capitalism in Russia*. But "What Is to Be Done?" is his first important statement of the organizational principles on which Bolshevism was to be founded. Although it is much concerned with various transitory controversies and does not foresee all the ramifications of the new model party, it established Lenin's uncompromising insistence on the maintenance of a uniform doctrine and a centralized, disciplined organization of professional revolutionists. Above all, it established his insistence on the direction of the masses by an elite guided by theory; the spontaneous strivings of the masses, he thought, could achieve nothing substantial. More than Lenin himself or his associates realized at the time, the pattern established in this essay was to leave its imprint on several generations of Russian political development. At the time it was published, however, it would not have seemed unreasonable to dismiss it as the vaporing of an intelligent, futile crank. Its author was only one of many political refugees from the Russian Empire, living with his wife in a single room rented from a German worker in Stuttgart. Here the fundamental work in the literature of Bolshevism was composed in a whispered voice, while its fanatically intense author paced the floor. It was completed in 1902 and published in Stuttgart as a pamphlet (in Russian) in March of that year.

W̲ithout a revolutionary theory there can be no revolutionary movement. This thought cannot be insisted upon too strongly at a time when

From "What Is to Be Done?" Lenin, *Selected Works* (Moscow: Foreign Languages Publishing House, 1950-1952), Vol. I, 203-409.

the fashionable preaching of opportunism goes hand in hand with an infatuation for the narrowest forms of practical activity. Yet, for Russian Social Democrats the importance of theory is enhanced by three more circumstances, which are often forgotten: firstly, by the fact that our Party is only in process of formation, its features are only just becoming outlined, and it is yet far from having settled accounts with other trends of revolutionary thought, which threaten to divert the movement from the correct path. On the contrary, precisely the very recent past was marked by a revival of non-Social Democratic revolutionary trends (which Axelrod [a founder of Russian Marxism—*ed.*] long ago warned the Economists would happen). Under these circumstances, what at first sight appears to be an "unimportant" mistake may lead to most deplorable consequences, and only shortsighted people can consider factional disputes and a strict differentiation between shades inopportune or superfluous. The fate of Russian Social Democracy for many, many years to come may depend on the strengthening of one or other "shade."

Secondly, the Social Democratic movement is in its very essence an international movement. This means not only that we must combat national chauvinism, but also that a movement that is starting in a young country can be successful only if it implements the experience of other countries. And in order to implement this experience, it is not enough merely to be acquainted with it, or simply to transcribe the latest resolutions. What it requires is the ability to treat this experience critically and to test it independently. Anybody who realizes how enormously the modern working-class movement has grown and branched out will understand what a reserve of theoretical forces and political (as well as revolutionary) experience is required to fulfill this task.

Thirdly, the national tasks of Russian Social Democracy are such as have never confronted any other socialist party in the world. Further on we shall have occasion to deal with the political and organizational duties which the task of emancipating the whole people from the yoke of autocracy imposes upon us. At this point, we only wish to state that the *role of vanguard fighter can be fulfilled only by a party that is guided by the most advanced theory*. In order to get some concrete understanding of what this means, let the reader recall such predecessors of Russian Social Democracy as Herzen, Belinsky, Chernyshevsky and the brilliant galaxy of revolutionaries of the Seventies; let him ponder over the world significance which Russian literature is now acquiring, let him . . . but that is enough! . . .

History has now confronted us with an immediate task which is the *most revolutionary* of all the *immediate* tasks that confront the proletariat of any country. The fulfilment of this task, the destruction of the most powerful bulwark, not only of European, but also (it may now be said) of Asiatic reaction, would make the Russian proletariat the vanguard of the international revolutionary proletariat. And we have the right to count upon acquiring this honorable title already earned by our predecessors, the revolutionaries of the Seventies, if we succeed in inspiring our movement—which is a thousand times broader and deeper —with the same devoted determination and vigor. . . .

In the previous chapter we pointed out how *universally* absorbed the educated youth of Russia was in the theories of Marxism in the middle of the Nineties. The strikes that followed the famous St. Petersburg industrial war of 1896 assumed a similar wholesale character. The fact that these strikes spread over the whole of Russia clearly showed how deep the newly awakening popular movement was, and if we are to speak of the "spontaneous element" then, of course, it is this movement which, first and foremost, must be regarded as spontaneous. But there is spontaneity and spontaneity. Strikes occurred in Russia in the Seventies and Sixties (and even in the first half of the nineteenth century), and were accompanied by the "spontaneous" destruction of machinery, etc. Compared with these "riots" the strikes of the Nineties might even be described as "conscious," to such an extent do they mark the progress which the working-class movement had made in that period. This shows that the "spontaneous element," in essence, represents nothing more nor less than consciousness in an *embryonic form*. Even the primitive riots expressed the awakening of consciousness to a certain extent: the workers were losing their agelong faith in the permanence of the system which oppressed them. They began . . . I shall not say to understand, but to sense the necessity for collective resistance, and definitely abandoned their slavish submission to their superiors. But this was, nevertheless, more in the nature of outbursts of desperation and vengeance than of *struggle*. The strikes of the Nineties revealed far greater flashes of consciousness: definite demands were advanced, the strike was carefully timed, known cases and examples in other places were discussed, etc. While the riots were simply revolts of the oppressed, the systematic strikes represented the class struggle in embryo, but only in embryo. Taken by themselves, these strikes were simply trade union struggles, but not yet Social Democratic struggles. They testified to the awakening antagonisms between workers and employers, but the workers were not, and could not be, conscious of the irreconcilable antagonism of their interests to the whole of the modern political and social system, i.e., theirs was not yet Social Democratic consciousness. In this sense, the strikes of the Nineties, in spite of the enormous progress they represented as compared with the "riots," remained a purely spontaneous movement.

We have said that *there could not yet be* Social Democratic consciousness among the workers. It could only be brought to them from without. The history of all countries shows that the working class, exclusively by its own effort, is able to develop only trade union consciousness, i.e., the conviction that it is necessary to combine in unions, fight the employers and strive to compel the government to pass necessary labour

legislation, etc. The theory of socialism, however, grew out of the philo-
sophic, historical and economic theories that were elaborated by the
educated representatives of the propertied classes, the intellectuals. According to their social status, the founders of modern scientific socialism,
Marx and Engels, themselves belonged to the bourgeois intelligentsia.
In the very same way, in Russia, the theoretical doctrine of Social Democracy arose quite independently of the spontaneous growth of the
working-class movement, it arose as a natural and inevitable outcome of
the development of ideas among the revolutionary socialist intelligentsia.
At the time of which we are speaking, i.e., the middle of the Nineties,
this doctrine not only represented the completely formulated program of
the Emancipation of Labour group, but had already won over to its
side the majority of the revolutionary youth in Russia.

Hence, we had both the spontaneous awakening of the masses of
the workers, the awakening to conscious life and conscious struggle,
and a revolutionary youth, armed with the Social Democratic theory,
eager to come into contact with the workers. . . .

And so, we have become convinced that the fundamental error committed by the "new trend" in Russian Social Democracy lies in its bow-
ing to spontaneity, and its failure to understand that the spontaneity
of the masses demands a mass of consciousness from us Social Democrats.
The greater the spontaneous upsurge of the masses, the more widespread
the movement becomes, so much the more rapidly, incomparably more
rapidly, grows the demand for greater consciousness in the theoretical,
political and organizational work of Social Democracy.

The spontaneous upsurge of the masses in Russia proceeded (and
continues) with such rapidity that the young Social Democrats proved
unprepared for these gigantic tasks. This unpreparedness is our common
misfortune, the misfortune of *all* Russian Social Democrats. The upsurge of the masses proceeded and spread uninterruptedly and with
continuity; it not only continued in the places where it began, but
spread to new localities and to new strata of the population (under the
influence of the working-class movement, there was a revival of ferment
among the students, the intellectuals generally and even among the
peasantry). Revolutionaries, however, *lagged behind* this upsurge both
in their "theories" and in their activity; they failed to establish an
uninterrupted organization having continuity with the past, and capable of *leading* the whole movement. . . .

The political struggle of Social Democracy is far more extensive and
complex than the economic struggle of the workers against the employers
and the government. Similarly (and indeed for that reason), the organization of a revolutionary Social Democratic party must inevitably be of a
different kind than the organizations of the workers designed for this
struggle. A workers' organization must in the first place be a trade organ-

ization; secondly, it must be as broad as possible; and thirdly, it must be as little clandestine as possible (here, and further on, of course, I have only autocratic Russia in mind). On the other hand, the organizations of revolutionaries must consist first, foremost and mainly of people who make revolutionary activity their profession (that is why I speak of organizations of *revolutionaries,* meaning revolutionary Social Democrats). In view of this common feature of the members of such an organization, *all distinctions as between workers and intellectuals,* and certainly distinctions of trade and profession, must be utterly *obliterated.* Such an organization must of necessity be not too extensive and as secret as possible. Let us examine this threefold distinction.

In countries where political liberty exists the distinction between a trade union and a political organization is clear enough, as is the distinction between trade unions and Social Democracy. The relation of the latter to the former will naturally vary in each country according to historical, legal and other conditions—it may be more or less close, complex, etc. (in our opinion it should be as close and simple as possible); but there can be no question of trade union organizations being identical with the Social Democratic party organizations in free countries. In Russia, however, the yoke of the autocracy appears at first glance to obliterate all distinctions between a Social Democratic organization and trade unions, because *all* workers' associations and *all* circles are prohibited, and because the principal manifestation and weapon of the workers' economic struggle—the strike—is regarded as a criminal (and sometimes even as a political!) offence. Conditions in our country, therefore, on the one hand, strongly "impel" the workers engaged in economic struggle to concern themselves with political questions, and, on the other, they "impel" Social Democrats to confuse trade unionism with Social Democracy. . . .

A small, compact core of the most reliable, experienced and hardened workers, with responsible representatives in the principal districts and connected by all the rules of strict secrecy with the organization of revolutionaries, can, with the widest support of the masses and without any formal organization, perform *all* the functions of a trade union organization, and perform them, moreover, in a manner desirable to Social Democracy. Only in this way can we secure the *consolidation* and development of a *Social Democratic* trade union movement, in spite of all the gendarmes.

It may be objected that an organization which is so loose that it is not even definitely formed, and which even has no enrolled and registered membership, cannot be called an organization at all. That may very well be. I am not out for names. But this "organization without members" will do everything that is required, and from the very outset guarantee the closest contact between our future trade unions and socialism. Only an incorrigible utopian would want a *broad* organization of workers, with elections, reports, universal suffrage, etc., under the autocracy.

The moral to be drawn from this is a simple one: if we begin with the solid foundation of a strong organization of revolutionaries, we can guarantee the stability of the movement as a whole and carry out the aims of both Social Democracy and of trade unions proper. If, however, we begin with a broad workers' organization, supposed to be most "accessible" to the masses (but as a matter of fact most accessible to the gendarmes and making the revolutionaries most accessible to the police), we shall achieve neither one nor the other of these aims; we shall not eliminate our amateurishness, and because we remain scattered and our forces are constantly broken up by the police, we shall only make the trade unions of the Zubatov and Ozerov [police-directed—ed.] type most accessible to the masses. . . .

I assert: 1) that no revolutionary movement can endure without a stable organization of leaders that maintains continuity; 2) that the wider the masses spontaneously drawn into the struggle, forming the basis of the movement and participating in it, the more urgent the need of such an organization, and the more solid this organization must be (for it is much easier for demagogues to sidetrack the more backward sections of the masses); 3) that such an organization must consist chiefly of people professionally engaged in revolutionary activity; 4) that in an autocratic state, the more we *confine* the membership of such an organization to people who are professionally engaged in revolutionary activity and who have been professionally trained in the art of combating the political police, the more difficult will it be to wipe out such an organization, and 5) the *greater* will be the number of people of the working class and of the other classes of society who will be able to join the movement and perform active work in it. . . .

Our chief sin with regard to organization is that *by our amateurishness we have lowered the prestige of revolutionaries in Russia.* A person who is flabby and shaky in questions of theory, who has a narrow outlook, who pleads the spontaneity of the masses as an excuse for his own sluggishness, who resembles a trade union secretary more than a people's tribune, who is unable to conceive of a broad and bold plan that would command the respect even of opponents, and who is inexperienced and clumsy in his own professional art—the art of combating the political police—why, such a man is not a revolutionary but a wretched amateur!

Let no active worker take offence at these frank remarks, for as far as insufficient training is concerned, I apply them first and foremost to myself. I used to work in a circle that set itself very wide, all-embracing tasks; and all of us, members of that circle, suffered painfully, acutely from the realization that we were proving ourselves to be amateurs at a moment in history when we might have been able to say, paraphrasing a well-known epigram: "Give us an organization of revolutionaries, and we shall overturn Russia!" And the more I recall the burning sense of shame I then experienced, the more bitter are my feelings towards those pseudo Social Democrats whose teachings "bring disgrace on the calling of a revolutionary," who fail to understand that our task is not to champion the degrading of the revolutionary to the level of an amateur, but to *raise* the amateurs to the level of revolutionaries.

ONE STEP FORWARD,
TWO STEPS BACK

There is no better proof of Lenin's arrogant self-assurance than his reaction to the events of the Second Congress (and the first substantial meeting) of the Russian Social Democratic Labor Party. All his efforts since 1900 had been bent toward this formative assembly, and his work on the newspaper *Iskra* (*The Spark*) had been directed toward the immediate goal of the Congress. But when Lenin failed to impose his vision of the model party upon the majority of the other revolutionists, he unhesitatingly seceded from the organization established by the Congress and from the editorial board of his beloved *Iskra*. In doing this he maintained that he was leading the *majority* of the newly founded party (in Russian, *bol'shinstvo* means "majority"; Bol'shevik means a member of the majority," hence the name of Lenin's party). It is true that Lenin had won a crucial vote on the regulations defining membership in the party and another on the composition of the editorial board *Iskra*. But these victories had been possible only after the withdrawal of a number of delegates from the Congress, and some of Lenin's adherents during the meetings, notably Plekhanov, withdrew their support soon afterwards.

In December, 1903, only four months after the close of the Congress, Lenin felt obliged to leave the editorial board of *Iskra* and establish a new organ, *Vperëd* (*Forward*), to speak authoritatively for his branch of the divided Social Democrats. His first major statement on the split in the party was the brochure, "One Step Forward, Two Steps Back," from which the following excerpt is drawn. It was originally published in Geneva in May, 1904.

Our party congress was unique and unprecedented in the entire history of the Russian revolutionary movement. For the first time a secret revolutionary party succeeded in emerging from the darkness of underground life into broad daylight, displaying to the world the whole course and outcome of the struggle within our party, the whole nature of our party

From "One Step Forward, Two Steps Back." Lenin, *Selected Works*, Vol. I, Part I, 410-656.

and of each of its more or less noticeable sections on questions of program, tactics and organization. For the first time we succeeded in throwing off the traditions of circle looseness and revolutionary philistinism, in bringing together dozens of the most varied groups, many of which had been fiercely warring among themselves and had been linked together solely by the force of an idea and were prepared (in principle, that is) to sacrifice all their group aloofness and group independence for the sake of the great whole which we were for the first time actually creating—the *party*. But in politics sacrifices are not obtained gratis, they have to be won in battle. The battle over the slaughter of the organizations was bound to be terribly fierce. The fresh breeze of free and open struggle blew into a gale. The gale swept away—and a good thing that it did!—every conceivable remnant of the circle interests, sentiments and traditions without exception, and for the first time created authoritative bodies that were really party bodies.

But it is one thing to call oneself something, and another to be it. It is one thing to sacrifice the circle system in principle for the sake of the party, and another to renounce one's own circle. The fresh breeze proved to be as yet too fresh for those who were used to musty philistinism. "The party was unable to stand the strain of its first congress," as Comrade Martov rightly put it (inadvertently) in his "Once More in the Minority." The sense of injury over the slaughter of the organizations was too strong. The furious gale raised all the mud from the bottom of our party stream; and the mud took its revenge. The old hidebound circle spirit overpowered the still young party spirit. The opportunist wing of the party, utterly routed though it had been, gained—temporarily, of course—the upper hand over the revolutionary wing.

The result is the new *Iskra* which is compelled to develop and deepen the error its editors committed at the party congress. The old *Iskra* taught the truths of revolutionary struggle. The new *Iskra* teaches the worldly wisdom of yielding and living in harmony with everyone. The old *Iskra* was the organ of militant orthodoxy. The new *Iskra* treats us to a recrudescence of opportunism—chiefly on questions of organization. The old *Iskra* earned the honor of being disliked by the opportunists, both Russian and West-European. The new *Iskra* has "grown wise" and will soon cease to be ashamed of the praises lavished on it by the extreme opportunists. The old *Iskra* marched unswervingly towards its goal, and there was no discrepancy between its word and its deed. The inherent falsity of the position of the new *Iskra* inevitably leads—independently even of anyone's will or intention—to political hypocrisy. It cries out against the circle spirit in order to conceal the victory of the circle spirit over the party spirit. It pharisaically condemns splits, as if one can imagine any way of avoiding splits in any at all organized party worthy of the name except by the subordination of the minority to the majority. It says that heed must be paid to revolutionary public opinion yet, while concealing the praises of the Akimovs [V. P. Akimov, who advocated economic, not political, struggle—*ed.*], it indulges in petty scandalmongering about the committees of the revolutionary wing of the party. How shameful! How they have disgraced our old *Iskra!*

One step forward, two steps back. . . . It happens in the lives of individuals, and it happens in the history of nations and in the development of parties. It would be the greatest criminal cowardice to doubt even for a moment the inevitable and complete triumph of the principles of revolutionary Social Democracy, of proletarian organization and party discipline. We have already won a great deal, and we must go on fighting, without being discouraged by reverses, fighting steadfastly, scorning the philistine methods of circle scrapping, doing our very utmost to preserve the single party tie among all the Russian Social Democrats which has been established at the cost of so much effort, and striving by dint of stubborn and systematic work to make all party members, and the workers in particular, fully and intelligently acquainted with the duties of party members, with the struggle at the Second Party Congress, with all the causes and all the stages of our disagreements, and with the utter disastrousness of opportunism, which, in the sphere of organization, as in the sphere of our program and our tactics, helplessly surrenders to the bourgeois psychology, uncritically adopts the point of view of bourgeois democracy, and blunts the weapon of the class struggle of the proletariat.

In its struggle for power the proletariat has no other weapon but organization. Disunited by the rule of anarchic competition in the bourgeois world, ground down by forced labour for capital, constantly thrust back to the "lower depths" of utter destitution, savagery and degeneration, the proletariat can become, and inevitably will become, an invincible force only when its ideological unification by the principles of Marxism is consolidated by the material unity of an organization which will weld millions of toilers into an army of the working class. Neither the decrepit rule of Russian tsardom, nor the senile rule of international capital will be able to withstand this army. Its ranks will become more and more serried, in spite of all zigzags and backward steps, in spite of the opportunist phrasemongering of the Girondists [moderate Jacobins in the French Revolution—*ed.*] of present-day Social Democracy, in spite of the smug praise of the antiquated circle spirit, and in spite of the tinsel and fuss of *intellectual* anarchism.

TWO TACTICS OF SOCIAL DEMOCRACY IN THE DEMOCRATIC REVOLUTION

While Lenin and most of the other Russian revolutionary leaders were quarreling over the organization of the party, the tsarist order began to disintegrate under the stress of the Russo-Japanese War, which started in 1904. Without much guidance from any of the revolutionary parties, the uprising gained strength throughout 1905, reaching its climax in the period October-December. At this point the régime succeeded in reversing the tide through a combination of relatively liberal concessions and effective use of military force.

Although Lenin had feared such an outcome and although he realized that his organizational work in the party was far from complete, he could not help but wish for the success of the revolution. But what did "success" mean? There was a wide difference of opinion on this question within the spectrum of the Russian political parties, and Lenin characteristically felt the need of establishing a distinct, "true" Bolshevik line. Although he was eager to return to Russia and to take an active part in the struggle, Lenin was unwilling to do so without fulfilling this obligation to theory, which he attempted in the brochure from which the following excerpt is taken. In "Two Tactics of Social Democracy in the Democratic Revolution," (published in Geneva, August, 1905), Lenin looked beyond the overthrow of tsarism, which he associates with the "feudal" stage of history, and attempted to chart the proper course for Marxists in an admittedly ambiguous situation. Lenin was too orthodox a Marxist at this time to expect that Russia could pass immediately from *feudalism* to *socialism,* yet the potentialities for really radical change, beyond the purely "bourgeois-democratic" level, seemed tempting to him. The result was an exercise in theory that never produced an immediate practical result (the revolution was suppressed by the end of 1905) but is worth reading for the light it casts on Lenin's approach to revolution in Russia. Three elements stand out: his emphasis on the revolutionary potential of the peasantry in Russia; his hope that a proletarian-peasant revolution in Russia may ignite a strictly socialist revolution in the West, the expected focus of proletarian upheaval; and his zeal to install a proletarian-peasant *dictatorship,* not a bourgeois-liberal régime, after the fall of the supposedly feudal order in Russia.

The degree of economic development of Russia (an objective condition) and the degree of class consciousness and organization of the broad masses of the proletariat (a subjective condition inseparably connected with the objective condition) make the immediate complete emancipation of the working class impossible. Only the most ignorant people can ignore the bourgeois nature of the democratic revolution which is now taking place; only the most naive optimists can forget how little as yet the masses of the workers are informed about the aims of socialism and about the methods of achieving it. And we are all convinced that the emancipation of the workers can be effected only by the workers themselves; a socialist revolution is out of the question unless the masses become class-conscious and organized, trained and educated in open class struggle against the entire bourgeoisie. In answer to the anarchist objections that we are putting off the socialist revolution, we say: we are not putting it off, but we are taking the first step towards it in the only possible way, along the only correct road, namely, the road of a democratic republic. Whoever wants to reach socialism by a different road, other than that of political democracy, will inevitably arrive at conclusions that are absurd and reactionary both in the economic and the political sense. If any workers ask us at the given moment why we should not go ahead and carry out our maximum program, we shall answer by pointing out how far the masses of the democratically-minded people still are from socialism, how undeveloped class antagonisms still are, how unorganized the proletarians still are. Organize hundreds of thousands of workers all over Russia; enlist the sympathy of millions for our program! Try to do this without confining yourselves to high-sounding but hollow anarchist phrases—and you will see at once that in order to achieve this organization, in order to spread this socialist enlightenment, we must achieve the fullest possible measure of democratic reforms.

Let us proceed further. Once we are clear about the importance of a provisional revolutionary government and the attitude of the proletariat toward it, the following question arises: is it permissible for us to participate in it (action from above) and, if so, under what conditions? What should be our action from below? The resolution supplies precise answers to both these questions. It emphatically declares that it is *per-*

From "Two Tactics of Social Democracy in the Democratic Revolution." Lenin, *Selected Works,* Vol. I, Part II, 11-151.

missible in principle for Social Democrats to participate in a provisional revolutionary government (during the period of a democratic revolution, the period of struggle for a republic). . . .

A change in the economic and political system in Russia along bourgeois-democratic lines is inevitable and unavoidable. No power on earth can prevent such a change. But the combined actions of the existing forces which are effecting that change may result in one of two things, may bring about one of two forms of that change. Either 1) the result will be a "decisive victory of the revolution over tsarism," or 2) the forces will be inadequate for a decisive victory and the matter will end in a deal between tsarism and the most "inconsistent" and most "self-seeking" elements of the bourgeoisie. All the infinite variety of detail and combinations, which no one is able to foresee, reduce themselves—in general and on the whole—to either the one or the other of these two outcomes. . . .

. . . the only force capable of gaining "a decisive victory over tsarism," is the *people*, i.e., the proletariat and the peasantry, if we take the main, big forces and distribute the rural and urban petty bourgeoisie (also part of "the people") between the two. "A decisive victory of the revolution over tsarism" is the *revolutionary-democratic dictatorship of the proletariat and the peasantry*. Our new *Iskra*-ists cannot escape from this conclusion, which *Vperëd* pointed out long ago. No one else is capable of gaining a decisive victory over tsarism.

And such a victory will be precisely a dictatorship, i.e., it must inevitably rely on military force, on the arming of the masses, on an insurrection, and not on institutions of one kind or another, established in a "lawful" or "peaceful" way. It can be only a dictatorship, for the realization of the changes which are urgently and absolutely indispensable for the proletariat and the peasantry will call forth the desperate resistance of the landlords, of the big bourgeoisie and of tsarism. Without a dictatorship it is impossible to break down that resistance and to repel the counterrevolutionary attempts. But of course it will be a democratic, not a socialist dictatorship. It will not be able (without a series of intermediary stages of revolutionary development) to affect the foundations of capitalism. At best it may bring about a radical redistribution of landed property in favour of the peasantry, establish consistent and full democracy including the formation of a republic, eradicate all the oppressive features of Asiatic bondage, not only in village but also in factory life, lay the foundation for a thorough improvement in the position of the workers and for a rise in their standard of living, and—last but not least—carry the revolutionary conflagration into Europe. Such a victory will by no means as yet transform our bourgeois revolution into a socialist revolution: the democratic revolution will not directly overstep the bounds of bourgeois social and economic relationships; nevertheless, the significance of such a victory for the future development of Russia and of the whole world will be immense. Nothing will raise the revolutionary energy of the world proletariat so much, nothing will shorten the path leading to its complete victory to such an extent, as this decisive victory of the revolution that has now started in Russia.

How far such a victory is probable is another question. We are not in the least inclined to be unreasonably optimistic on that score, we do not for a moment forget the immense difficulties of this task, but since we are out to fight we must desire victory and be able to point out the right road to it. Tendencies capable of leading to such a victory undoubtedly exist. True, our, Social Democratic, influence on the masses of the proletariat is as yet very, very inadequate; the revolutionary influence on the mass of the peasantry is altogether insignificant; the proletariat, and especially the peasantry, are still frightfully scattered, backward and ignorant. But revolution unites quickly and enlightens quickly. Every step in its development rouses the masses and attracts them with irresistible force to the side of the revolutionary program, as the only program that fully and consistently expresses their real and vital interests. . . .

The bourgeoisie, in the mass, will inevitably turn towards counter-revolution, towards the autocracy, against the revolution and against the people, immediately its narrow, selfish interests are met, immediately it "recoils" from consistent democracy (*and it is already recoiling from it!*). There remains the "people," that is, the proletariat and the peasantry: the proletariat alone can be relied on to march to the end, for it is going far beyond the democratic revolution. That is why the proletariat fights in the front ranks for a republic and contemptuously rejects silly and unworthy advice to take care not to frighten away the bourgeoisie. The peasantry includes a great number of semiproletarian as well as petty-bourgeois elements. This causes it also to be unstable and compels the proletariat to unite in a strictly class party. But the instability of the peasantry differs radically from the instability of the bourgeoisie, for at the present time the peasantry is interested not so much in the absolute preservation of private property as in the confiscation of the landed estates, one of the principal forms of private property. While this does not make the peasantry become socialist or cease to be petty-bourgeois, it is capable of becoming a wholehearted and most radical adherent of the democratic revolution. The peasantry will inevitably become such if only the progress of revolutionary events, which is enlightening it, is not checked too soon by the treachery of the bourgeoisie and the defeat of the proletariat. Subject to this condition, the peasantry will inevitably become a bulwark of the revolution and the republic, for only a completely victorious revolution can give the peasantry *everything* in the sphere of agrarian reforms—*everything* that the peasants desire, of which they dream, and of which they truly stand in need . . . in order to emerge from the mire of semiserfdom, from the gloom of oppression and servitude, in order to improve their living conditions as much as it is possible to improve them under the system of commodity production. . , .

The proletariat must carry to completion the democratic revolution, by allying to itself the mass of the peasantry in order to crush by force the resistance of the autocracy and to paralyze the instability of the bourgeoisie. The proletariat must accomplish the socialist revolution, by allying to itself the mass of the semiproletarian elements of the population in order to crush by force the resistance of the bourgeoisie and to paralyze the instability of the peasantry and the petty bourgeoisie. Such are the tasks of the proletariat, which the new *Iskra*-ists present so narrowly in all their arguments and resolutions about the sweep of the revolution. . . .

Revolutions are the locomotives of history, said Marx. Revolutions are the festivals of the oppressed and the exploited. At no other time are the masses of the people in a position to come forward so actively as creators of a new social order as at a time of revolution. At such times the people are capable of performing miracles, if judged by the narrow, philistine scale of gradual progress. But the leaders of the revolutionary parties must also make their aims more comprehensive and bold at such a time, so that their slogans shall always be in advance of the revolutionary initiative of the masses, serve as a beacon, reveal to them our democratic and socialist ideal in all its magnitude and splendor and show them the shortest and most direct route to complete, absolute and decisive victory. Let us leave to the opportunists of the *Osvobozhdeniye* [*Liberation,* a liberal newspaper—*ed.*] bourgeoisie the task of inventing roundabout, circuitous paths of compromise out of fear of the revolution and of the direct path. If we are compelled by force to drag ourselves along such paths, we shall be able to fulfill our duty in petty, everyday work also. But let ruthless struggle first decide the choice of the path. We shall be traitors to and betrayers of the revolution if we do not use this festive energy of the masses and their revolutionary ardor to wage a ruthless and self-sacrificing struggle for the direct and decisive path. Let the bourgeois opportunists contemplate the future reaction with craven fear. The workers will not be frightened either by the thought that the reaction promises to be terrible or by the thought that the bourgeoisie proposes to recoil. The workers are not looking forward to striking bargains, are not asking for sops; they are striving to crush the reactionary forces without mercy, i.e., to set up the *revolutionary-democratic dictatorship of the proletariat and the peasantry.* . . .

At the head of the whole of the people, and particularly of the peasantry—for complete freedom, for a consistent democratic revolution, for a republic! At the head of all the toilers and the exploited—for socialism! Such must in practice be the policy of the revolutionary proletariat, such is the class slogan which must permeate and determine the solution of every tactical problem, of every practical step of the workers' party during the revolution.

THE WAR AND RUSSIAN
SOCIAL DEMOCRACY

Lenin was never more isolated and never more determined than at the onset of the First World War in 1914. His isolation was both geographical and political, for he was forced to live in Switzerland, cut off from Russia by the war, and his attitude toward the war set him apart from the majority of Social Democrats. Despite the efforts of the Second International, a league of European socialist parties, to provide machinery for the prevention of war, they were unable to avert the disaster of August, 1914, and the great majority of socialists from England to Russia took a patriotic line of support for their country's war effort. Among the socialists who supported their respective war efforts were Karl Kautsky, the German Social Democratic leader who had formerly been Lenin's chief hero among western socialists, and Plekhanov, the founder of Russian Marxism and a Menshevik Social Democrat after 1903. No "bourgeois" liberal nor even a tsarist general ever evoked from Lenin such venomous scorn as he directed at these "traitors" to socialism.

The following excerpt from "The War and Russian Social Democracy" illustrates his prolific production of polemics on this subject, all of which are based on his "theses" on the war, written in October, 1914. The present article, in some ways more convenient than the "theses," was written in October and published in Switzerland in the Russian newspaper *Sotsial-Demokrat* in November 1914.

The European war, for which the governments and the bourgeois parties of all countries have been preparing for decades, has broken out. The growth of armaments, the extreme intensification of the struggle for markets in the epoch of the latest, the imperialist, stage of capitalist development in the advanced countries, and the dynastic interests of the most backward East European monarchies were inevitably bound to lead, and have led, to this war. Seizure of territory and subjugation of foreign nations, ruin of a competing nation and plunder of its wealth, diverting the attention of the working masses from the internal political crises in Rus-

From "The War and Russian Social Democracy." Lenin, *Selected Works*, Vol. I, Part II, 397-406.

sia, Germany, England and other countries, disuniting and nationalist doping of the workers and the extermination of their vanguard with the object of weakening the revolutionary movement of the proletariat—such is the only real meaning, substance and significance of the present war.

On Social Democracy, primarily, rests the duty of disclosing this true meaning of the war and of ruthlessly exposing the falsehood, sophistry and "patriotic" phrase-mongering spread by the ruling classes, the land-lords and the bourgeoisie, in defence of the war.

At the head of one group of belligerent nations stands the German bourgeoisie. It is fooling the working class and the laboring masses by asserting that it is waging war in defence of the fatherland, freedom and civilization, for the liberation of the peoples oppressed by tsardom, for the destruction of reactionary tsardom. But, as a matter of fact, this bourgeoisie, which servilely grovels before the Prussian Junkers, headed by Wilhelm II, has always been a most faithful ally of tsardom and an enemy of the revolutionary movement of the workers and peasants of Russia. In reality, whatever the outcome of the war may be, this bourgeoisie will, together with the Junkers, exert every effort to support the tsarist monarchy against a revolution in Russia. . . .

The other group of belligerent nations is headed by the British and French bourgeoisie, which is fooling the working class and the laboring masses by asserting that it is waging a war for the defence of their countries, for freedom and civilization against the militarism and despotism of Germany. But, as a matter of fact, this bourgeoisie has long been using its billions to hire the armies of Russian tsardom, the most reactionary and barbarous monarchy in Europe, and to prepare them for an attack on Germany.

In reality, the object of the struggle of the British and French bourgeoisie is to seize the German colonies and to ruin a competing nation which is distinguished for its more rapid economic development. And, in pursuit of this noble aim, the "advanced" "democratic" nations are helping the savage tsarist regime to draw the noose tighter around Poland, the Ukraine, etc., and to crush the revolution in Russia more thoroughly.

Neither of the two groups of belligerent countries lags behind the other in robbery, atrocities and the infinite brutalities of war; but in order to fool the proletariat and distract its attention from the only real war of liberation, namely, a civil war against the bourgeoisie both of "its own" and of "foreign" countries, in order to further this lofty aim, the bourgeoisie of each country is trying with the help of lying talk about patriotism to extol the significance of its "own" national war and asserts that it is not striving to vanquish the enemy for the sake of plunder and the seizure of territory, but for the sake of "liberating" all other peoples, except its own.

But the more zealously the governments and the bourgeoisie of all countries strive to divide the workers and to pit them against each other, and the more ferociously they employ martial law and military censorship (which even now, in time of war, are applied more stringently against the "internal" than against the foreign enemy) for this lofty purpose, the more urgently is it the duty of the class-conscious proletariat to preserve its class solidarity, its internationalism, its socialist convictions from the orgy of chauvinism of the "patriotic" bourgeois cliques of all countries. The renunciation of this task would mean the renunciation by the class-conscious workers of all their emancipatory and democratic, not to mention socialist, aspirations.

It is with a feeling of deepest chagrin that we have to record that the socialist parties of the leading European countries have not discharged this duty, while the behavior of the leaders of these parties—particularly of the German—borders on downright betrayal of the cause of socialism. At this moment of supreme world-historical importance, the majority of the leaders of the present, the Second (1889-1914), Socialist International are trying to substitute nationalism for socialism. Owing to their behavior, the workers' parties of these countries did not oppose the criminal conduct of the governments but called upon the working class to *identify* its position with that of the imperialist governments. The leaders of the International committed an act of treachery towards socialism in voting for war credits, in seconding the chauvinist ("patriotic") slogans of the bourgeoisie of their "own" countries, in justifying and defending war, in entering the bourgeois Cabinets of belligerent countries, etc., etc. The most influential socialist leaders, and the most influential organs of the socialist press of present-day Europe, hold chauvinistic bourgeois and liberal views, and not socialist views. The responsibility for disgracing socialism in this way rests primarily on the German Social Democrats, who were the strongest and most influential party in the Second International. But neither can one justify the French Socialists, who accepted ministerial posts in the government of the very bourgeoisie which betrayed its country and allied itself with Bismarck to crush the Commune. . . .

Under present conditions, it is impossible to determine, from the standpoint of the international proletariat, the defeat of which of the two groups of belligerent nations would be the lesser evil for socialism. But for us, the Russian Social Democrats, there cannot be the slightest doubt that from the standpoint of the working class and of the laboring masses of all the nations of Russia, the lesser evil would be the defeat of the tsarist monarchy, the most reactionary and barbarous of governments, which is oppressing the greatest number of nations and the largest mass of the population of Europe and Asia. . . .

The transformation of the present imperialist war into a civil war is the only correct proletarian slogan; it was indicated by the experience of the Commune and outlined by the Basle resolution (1912), and it logically follows from all the conditions of an imperialist war among highly developed bourgeois countries. However difficult such a transformation may appear at any given moment, Socialists will never relinquish systematic, persistent and undeviating preparatory work in this direction once war has become a fact.

Only in this way can the proletariat shake off its dependence on the chauvinist bourgeoisie, and, in one form or another, more or less rapidly, take decisive steps towards the real freedom of nations and towards Socialism.

Long live the international fraternity of the workers against the chauvinism and patriotism of the bourgeoisie of all countries!

Long live a proletarian International, freed from opportunism!

IMPERIALISM: THE HIGHEST STAGE
OF CAPITALISM

Along with his pamphleteering and politicking against "social chauvinism," Lenin found time during his wartime confinement in Switzerland to return to matters of basic theory. The outcome was his second major economic study, "Imperialism: The Highest Stage of Capitalism" (the first, *The Development of Capitalism in Russia,* was also written in confinement—the more stringent confinement of prison and Siberian exile). Lenin had reviled numerous Socialists for their "revisionism." A revisionist was one who held that Marx had not foreseen some of the most salient developments in the economic and political future of Europe; for this reason, it was held necessary to modify his teachings in the light of experience. Lenin had considered such treatment of Marxian theory to be treasonous, but his own study of imperialism was in essence a major "revision" of classical Marxism. When Marx died in 1883 the late-nineteenth century race for colonial expansion was just beginning, and Marx had not paid much attention to this activity in formulating his major theories. But, in the light of subsequent events and under the influence of the writing of the English economist Hobson, Lenin held that the "imperialist" development of capitalism was in fact a major historical epoch. In the imperialist stage of history, Lenin believed, capitalism extended its life expectancy by expanding into the underdeveloped areas of the world; but at the same time capitalism guaranteed its final downfall by creating new stresses within itself, notably the antagonism of competing imperialists and the hatred of colonial peoples for the foreign exploiters. All of this was not explicitly worked out in "Imperialism" but the booklet provided the basic theory on which later, more explicit tracts developed the revolutionary importance of the colonial world.

While the socialists who are usually called revisionists tended to replace the prophecy of revolutionary change with one of parliamentary and labor-union reform, Lenin's own "revisionism" represented a re-enforcement of the tough side of Marxian theory. It attempted to explain why the proletarian revolution in Europe, expected by Marx as early as 1848, had failed to materialize by 1916, and it assured the inevitable coming of such a revolution.

Although Lenin's booklet was written between January and

July, 1916, he was unable to publish it until his return to Russia in April of the following year.

We have seen that in its economic essence imperialism is monopoly capitalism. This in itself determines its place in history, for monopoly that grows out of the soil of free competition, and precisely out of free competition, is the transition from the capitalist system to a higher social economic order. We must take special note of the four principal types of monopoly, or principal manifestations of monopoly capitalism, which are characteristic of the epoch we are examining.

Firstly, monopoly arose out of a very high stage of development of the concentration of production. This refers to the monopolist capitalist combines, cartels, syndicates and trusts. We have seen the important part these play in present-day economic life. At the beginning of the twentieth century, monopolies had acquired complete supremacy in the advanced countries, and although the first steps towards the formation of the cartels were first taken by countries enjoying the protection of high tariffs (Germany, America), Great Britain, with her system of free trade, revealed the same basic phenomenon, only a little later, namely the birth of monopoly out of the concentration of production.

Secondly, monopolies have stimulated the seizure of the most important sources of raw materials, especially for the basic and most highly cartelized industries in capitalist society: the coal and iron industries. The monopoly of the most important sources of raw materials has enormously increased the power of big capital, and has sharpened the antagonism between cartelized and non-cartelized industry.

Thirdly, monopoly has sprung from the banks. The banks have developed from humble middlemen enterprises into the monopolists of finance capital. Some three to five of the biggest banks in each of the foremost capitalist countries have achieved the "personal union" of industrial and bank capital, and have concentrated in their hands the control of thousands upon thousands of millions which form the greater part of the capital and income of entire countries. A financial oligarchy, which throws a close network of dependence relationships over all the economic and political institutions of present-day bourgeois society without exception—such is the most striking manifestation of this monopoly.

Fourthly, monopoly has grown out of colonial policy. To the numerous "old" motives of colonial policy, finance capital has added the struggle for the sources of raw materials, for the export of capital, for "spheres of influence," i.e., for spheres for profitable deals, concessions, monopolist profits and so on, and finally, for economic territory in general. When

From "Imperialism: The Highest Stage of Capitalism." Lenin, *Selected Works*, Vol. I, Part II, 433-568.

the colonies of the European powers in Africa, for instance, comprised only one-tenth of that territory (as was the case in 1876), colonial policy was able to develop by methods other than those of monopoly—by the "free grabbing" of territories, so to speak. But when nine-tenths of Africa had been seized (by 1900), when the whole world had been divided up, there was inevitably ushered in the era of monopoly ownership of colonies and, consequently, of particularly intense struggle for the division and the redivision of the world.

The extent to which monopolist capital has intensified all the contradictions of capitalism is generally known. It is sufficient to mention the high cost of living and the tyranny of the cartels. This intensification of contradictions constitutes the most powerful driving force of the transitional period of history, which began from the time of the final victory of world finance capital.

Monopolies, oligarchy, the striving for domination instead of striving for liberty, the exploitation of an increasing number of small or weak nations by a handful of the richest or most powerful nations—all these have given birth to those distinctive characteristics of imperialism which compel us to define it as parasitic or decaying capitalism. More and more prominently there emerges, as one of the tendencies of imperialism, the creation of the "rentier state," the usurer state, in which the bourgeoisie to an ever increasing degree lives on the proceeds of capital exports and by "clipping coupons." It would be a mistake to believe that this tendency to decay precludes the rapid growth of capitalism. It does not. In the epoch of imperialism, certain branches of industry, certain strata of the bourgeoisie and certain countries betray, to a greater or lesser degree, now one and now another of these tendencies. On the whole, capitalism is growing far more rapidly than before; but this growth is not only becoming more and more uneven in general, its unevenness also manifests itself, in particular, in the decay of the countries which are richest in capital (England). . . .

The receipt of high monopoly profits by the capitalists in one of the numerous branches of industry, in one of the numerous countries, etc., makes it economically possible for them to bribe certain sections of the workers, and for a time a fairly considerable minority of them, and win them to the side of the bourgeoisie of a given industry or given nation against all the others. The intensification of antagonisms between imperialist nations for the division of the world increases this striving. And so there is created that bond between imperialism and opportunism, which revealed itself first and most clearly in England, owing to the fact that certain features of imperialist development were observable there much earlier than in other countries. Some writers, L. Martov [Y. O. Martov, leader of Mensheviks—*ed.*], for example, are prone to wave aside the connection between imperialism and opportunism in the working-class movement—a particularly glaring fact at the present time—by resorting to "official optimism" (à la Kautsky and Huysmans) [Huysmans was the secretary of the Second International—*ed*.] like the following: the cause of the opponents of capitalism would be hopeless if it were precisely progressive capitalism that led to the increase of opportunism, or, if it were precisely the best paid workers who were inclined towards opportunism, etc. We must have no illusions about "optimism" of this kind. It is optimism in regard to opportunism; it is optimism which serves to conceal opportunism. As a matter of fact the extraordinary rapidity and the particularly revolting character of the development of opportunism is by no means a guarantee that its victory will be durable: the rapid growth of a malignant abscess on a healthy body can only cause it to burst more quickly and thus relieve the body of it. The most dangerous of all in this respect are those who do not wish to understand that the fight against imperialism is a sham and humbug unless it is inseparably bound up with the fight against opportunism.

From all that has been said in this book on the economic essence of imperialism, it follows that we must define it as capitalism in transition, or, more precisely, as moribund capitalism. It is very instructive in this respect to note that the bourgeois economists, in describing modern capitalism, frequently employ catchwords and phrases like "interlocking," "absence of isolation," etc.; "in conformity with their functions and course of development," banks are "not purely private business enterprises; they are more and more outgrowing the sphere of purely private business regulation." And this very Riesser [a non-Marxist German economist—*ed*.], who uttered the words just quoted, declares with all seriousness that the "prophecy" of the Marxists concerning "socialization" has "not come true"!

What then does this catchword "interlocking" express? It merely expresses the most striking feature of the process going on before our eyes. It shows that the observer counts the separate trees, but cannot see the wood. It slavishly copies the superficial, the fortuitous, the chaotic. It reveals the observer as one who is overwhelmed by the mass of raw material and is utterly incapable of appreciating its meaning and importance. Ownership of shares, the relations between owners of private property "interlock in a haphazard way." But underlying this interlocking, its very base, is the changing social relations of production. When a big enterprise assumes gigantic proportions, and, on the basis of an exact computation of mass data, organizes according to plan the supply of primary raw materials to the extent of two-thirds, or three-fourths of all that is necessary for tens of millions of people; when the raw materials are transported in a systematic and organized manner to the most suitable place of production, sometimes hundreds or thousands of miles, when a single center directs all the consecutive stages of work right up to the manufacture of numerous varieties of finished articles;

when these products are distributed according to a single plan among tens and hundreds of millions of consumers (the distribution of oil in America and Germany by the American "oil trust")—then it becomes evident that we have socialization of production, and not mere "interlocking"; that private economic and private property relations constitute a shell which no longer fits its contents, a shell which must inevitably decay if its removal by artificial means be delayed; a shell which may continue in a state of decay for a fairly long period (if, at the worst, the cure of the opportunist abscess is protracted), but which will inevitably be removed. . . .

ON THE TASKS OF THE
PROLETARIAT IN THE
PRESENT REVOLUTION

Lenin's dramatic return to Russia through Germany, by arrangement with the German General Staff, was followed by an equally dramatic political pronouncement, the "April Theses." In a sense, this statement was the climactic point in Lenin's career, the culminating moment in his long insistence on revolutionary "truth" and opposition to "heretical" compromise. When he arrived in Russia during the euphoric, fraternal period that followed the overthrow of tsarism in February [March, New Style] 1917 *, almost all political elements, from the liberals to the Bolsheviks, were acquiescent to at least a temporary truce under the joint rule of the Provisional Government and the Soviets of Workers, Soldiers, and Peasants. To Lenin, this compromising attitude was the worst mistake that the "true" friends of the proletariat could make, misleading the masses and diverting them from their historic mission.

To reverse this tendency, Lenin sallied forth on his first night in Petrograd, attempting to establish once again a distinct and uncompromising Bolshevik position at a time when many of his closest supporters in the party did not agree with him. On his second night, April 4 [April 17, New Style] Lenin presented ten major theses setting forth his position, and first published these on April 7 [April 20, New Style] in the Bolshevik newspaper *Pravda*, in an article entitled "On the Tasks of the Proletariat in the Present Revolution," from which the following excerpt is drawn. Lenin's nearly complete success in winning the party to his program within a few weeks and in carrying out a successful seizure of power eight months later seemed to vindicate his long record as an obstinate dogmatist and factionalist.

* Russia did not change from the "Old Style" or Julian calendar to the "New Style" or Gregorian (Western) calendar until February, 1918. In the twentieth century the Old Style runs thirteen days behind the New Style, to the confusion of everyone who deals with Russian history around the time of the Revolution.

I arrived in Petrograd only on the night of April 3 [April 16, New Style], and therefore at the meeting on April 4 [April 17, New Style] I could, of course, deliver the report on the tasks of the revolutionary proletariat only on my own behalf, and with reservations as to insufficient preparation.

The only thing I could do to facilitate matters for myself and for *honest* opponents was to prepare theses in writing. I read them, and gave the text to Comrade Tsereteli. I read them very slowly, and *twice*: first at a meeting of Bolsheviks and then at a meeting of both Bolsheviks and Mensheviks.

I publish these personal theses of mine with only the briefest explanatory notes, which were developed in far greater detail in the report.

THESES

1. In our attitude towards the war, which also under the new government of Lvov [Prince G. E. Lvov, premier of the Provisional Government—*ed.*] and Co. unquestionably remains on Russia's part a predatory imperialist war owing to the capitalist nature of that government, not the slightest concession to "revolutionary defencism" is permissible.

The class-conscious proletariat can give its consent to a revolutionary war, which would really justify revolutionary defencism, only on condition: a) that the power pass to the proletariat and the poor sections of the peasantry bordering on the proletariat; b) that all annexations be renounced in actual fact and not in word; c) that a complete break be effected in actual fact with all capitalist interests.

In view of the undoubted honesty of the broad strata of the mass believers in revolutionary defencism, who accept the war as a necessity only, and not as a means of conquest, in view of the fact that they are being deceived by the bourgeoisie, it is necessary with particular thoroughness, persistence and patience to explain their error to them, to explain the inseparable connection existing between capital and the imperialist war, and to prove that without overthrowing capital *it is impossible* to end the war by a truly democratic peace, a peace not imposed by violence.

The most widespread propaganda of this view in the army on active service must be organized.

Fraternization.

2. The specific feature of the present situation in Russia is that it represents a *transition* from the first stage of the revolution—which, owing to the insufficient class consciousness and organization of the proletariat, placed the power in the hands of the bourgeoisie—*to the*

second stage, which must place the power in the hands of the proletariat and the poorest strata of the peasantry.

This transition is characterized, on the one hand, by a maximum of legally recognized rights (Russia is *now* the freest of all the belligerent countries in the world); on the other, by the absence of violence in relation to the masses, and, finally, by the unreasoning confidence of the masses in the government of capitalists, the worst enemies of peace and socialism.

This peculiar situation demands of us an ability to adapt ourselves to the *special* conditions of party work among unprecedentedly large masses of proletarians who have just awakened to political life.

3. No support for the Provisional Government; the utter falsity of all its promises should be explained, particularly those relating to the renunciation of annexations. Exposure in place of the impermissible illusion-breeding "demand" that *this* government, a government of capitalists, should *cease* to be an imperialist government.

4. Recognition of the fact that in most of the Soviets of Workers' Deputies our party is in a minority, and so far in a small minority, as against *a bloc of all* the petty-bourgeois opportunist elements, who have yielded to the influence of the bourgeoisie and convey its influence to the proletariat, from the Popular Socialists and the Socialist Revolutionaries down to the Organization Committee (Chkheidze, Tsereteli, etc.), Steklov [the first two were Menshevik leaders of the Petrograd Soviet; the latter was neither a Bolshevik nor a Menshevik at this time—*ed.*], etc.

It must be explained to the masses that the Soviets of Workers' Deputies are the *only possible* form of the revolutionary government, and that therefore our task is, as long as *this* government yields to the influence of the bourgeoisie, to present a patient, systematic, and persistent *explanation* of the errors of their tactics, an explanation especially adapted to the practical needs of the masses.

As long as we are in the minority we carry on the work of criticizing and exposing errors and at the same time we preach the necessity of transferring the entire power of state to the Soviets of Workers' Deputies, so that the masses may by experience overcome their mistakes.

5. Not a parliamentary republic—to return to a parliamentary republic from the Soviets of Workers' Deputies would be a retrograde step—but a republic of Soviets of Workers', Agricultural Laborers' and Peasants' Deputies throughout the country, from top to bottom.

Abolition of the police, the army and the bureaucracy.

The salaries of all officials, all of whom are to be elected and to be subject to recall at any time, not to exceed the average wage of a competent worker.

6. In the agrarian program the most important part to be assigned to the Soviets of Agricultural Laborers' Deputies.

Confiscation of all landed estates.

Nationalization of *all* lands in the country, the disposal of the land to be put in the charge of the local Soviets of Agricultural Laborers' and Peasants' Deputies. The organization of separate Soviets of Deputies of Poor Peasants. The creation of model farms on each of the large estates (varying from 100 to 300 dessiatinas [one dessiatina equals 2.7 acres—*ed.*], in accordance with local and other conditions, by decisions of the local institutions) under the control of the Soviets of Agricultural Laborers' Deputies and for the public account.

7. The immediate amalgamation of all banks in the country into a single national bank, and the institution of control over it by the Soviets of Workers' Deputies.

8. It isn't our *immediate* task to "introduce" socialism, but only to bring social production and distribution of products at once under the *control* of the Soviets of Workers' Deputies.

9. Party tasks:

    a) Immediate convocation of a party congress;

    b) Alteration of the party program, mainly:

        1) On the question of imperialism and the imperialist war;

        2) On our attitude towards the state and *our* demand for a "commune state";

        3) Amendment of our antiquated minimum program.

    c) Change of the party's name.

10. A new International.

We must take the initiative in creating a revolutionary International, an International against the *social-chauvinists* and against the "Center." . . .

STATE AND REVOLUTION

In the midst of his struggle against the Provisional Government of 1917, unforeseen events forced Lenin to go into seclusion. In early July the collapse of the last Russian military offensive of the World War precipitated violent antiwar and antigovernment demonstrations in Petrograd. These failed by a narrow margin. The Provisional Government accused Lenin, who had for a time supported the demonstrations, of treasonous relations with the Germans, and to avoid prosecution he fled to Finland, which was relatively safe from the Petrograd government.

It is a remarkable demonstration of Lenin's penchant for theory that at a time when the political fate of Russia was at stake, he chose to devote himself to a reconsideration of the least practical of all the theoretical questions of Marxism: the transition from the evil society of the capitalist present to the virtuous society of the Communist future. Although Lenin's discussion of this problem reveals rather little about the Soviet Union as it actually emerged, it does illuminate clearly the essential two-sidedness of Lenin's character: his ruthless attitude toward existing enemies and his lofty conception of a future society of harmony and freedom—the justification for his acknowledged toughness in the present. In other words, Lenin follows the tradition of Marx in his sweeping condemnation of human nature as it is and his unlimited hopes for human nature as it might be.

Full of tedious polemics against contemporary "traitors" to Marxism, repetitious and overloaded with citations of Marxian classics, "State and Revolution" remains Lenin's most important confession of faith in the long-term cause to which he devoted his life. Perhaps it would have been more tightly organized and incisive if Lenin, who began research for the essay while in Switzerland in 1916, had not been interrupted during the writing of the work in 1917 by the oncoming Bolshevik revolution. This event was hardly a result of "State and Revolution," for the unfinished essay was not published (never to be completed) until early 1918, but the Bolshevik revolution did lend importance to "State and Revolution" by making its author one of the leading figures on the twentieth century.

Democracy for the vast majority of the people, and suppression by force, i.e., exclusion from democracy, of the exploiters and oppressors of the people—this is the change democracy undergoes during the *transition* from capitalism to communism.

Only in communist society, when the resistance of the capitalists has been completely crushed, when the capitalists have disappeared, when there are no classes (i.e., when there is no difference between the members of society as regards their relation to the social means of production), *only* then "the state . . . ceases to exist," and it *"becomes possible to speak of freedom."* Only then will there become possible and be realized a truly complete democracy, democracy without any exceptions whatever. And only then will democracy begin to *wither away*, owing to the simple fact that, freed from capitalist slavery, from the untold horrors, savagery, absurdities and infamies of capitalist exploitation, people will gradually *become accustomed* to observing the elementary rules of social intercourse that have been known for centuries and repeated for thousands of years in all copybook maxims; they will become accustomed to observing them without force, without compulsion, without subordination, *without the special apparatus* for compulsion which is called the state.

The expression "the state *withers away*" is very well chosen [by Marx—ed.], for it indicates both the gradual and the spontaneous nature of the process. Only habit can, and undoubtedly will, have such an effect; for we see around us on millions of occasions how readily people become accustomed to observing the necessary rules of social intercourse when there is no exploitation, when there is nothing that rouses indignation, nothing that evokes protest and revolt and creates the need for *suppression.* . . .

We have seen that the *Communist Manifesto* simply places side by side the two concepts: "to raise the proletariat to the position of the ruling class" and "to win the battle of democracy." On the basis of all that has been said above, it is possible to determine more precisely how democracy changes in the transition from capitalism to communism.

In capitalist society, providing it develops under the most favourable conditions, we have a more or less complete democracy in the democratic republic. But this democracy is always hemmed in by the narrow limits set by capitalist exploitation, and consequently always remains, in reality, a democracy for the minority, only for the propertied classes, only for the rich. Freedom in capitalist society always remains about the same as it was in the ancient Greek republics: freedom for the slaveowners. Owing to the conditions of capitalist exploitation the modern wage slaves are so crushed by want and poverty that "they cannot be bothered with democracy," "they cannot be bothered with politics"; in the ordinary peaceful course of events the majority of the population is debarred from participation in public and political life. . . .

Democracy for an insignificant minority, democracy for the rich—that is the democracy of capitalist society. If we look more closely into the machinery of capitalist democracy, we shall see everywhere, in the "petty" —supposedly petty—details of the suffrage (residential qualification, exclusion of women, etc.), in the technique of the representative institutions, in the actual obstacles to the right of assembly (public buildings are not for "beggars"!), in the purely capitalist organization of the daily press, etc., etc.—we shall see restriction after restriction upon democracy. These restrictions, exceptions, exclusions, obstacles for the poor, seem slight, especially in the eyes of one who has never known want himself and has never been in close contact with the oppressed classes in their mass life (and nine-tenths, if not ninety-nine hundredths, of the bourgeois publicists and politicians are of this category); but in their sum total these restrictions exclude and squeeze out the poor from politics, from active participation in democracy. . . .

But from this capitalist democracy—that is inevitably narrow, and stealthily pushes aside the poor, and is therefore hypocritical and false to the core—forward development does not proceed simply, directly and smoothly towards "greater and greater democracy," as the liberal professors and petty-bourgeois opportunists would have us believe. No, forward development, i.e., towards communism, proceeds through the dictatorship of the proletariat, and cannot do otherwise, for the *resistance* of the capitalist exploiters cannot be *broken* by anyone else or in any other way.

And the dictatorship of the proletariat, i.e., the organization of the vanguard of the oppressed as the ruling class for the purpose of suppressing the oppressors, cannot result merely in an expansion of democracy. *Simultaneously* with an immense expansion of democracy, which *for the first time* becomes democracy for the poor, democracy for the people, and not democracy for the moneybags, the dictatorship of the proletariat imposes a series of restrictions on the freedom of the oppressors, the exploiters, the capitalists. We must suppress them in order to free humanity from wage slavery, their resistance must be crushed by force; it is clear that where there is suppression, where there is violence, there is no freedom and no democracy. . . .

Furthermore, during the *transition* from capitalism to communism suppression is *still* necessary; but it is now the suppression of the exploiting minority by the exploited majority. A special apparatus, a special machine for suppression, the "state" is *still* necessary, but this is now a transitional state; it is no longer a state in the proper sense of the word; for the suppression of the minority *of yesterday* is comparatively so easy, simple and natural a task that it will entail far less bloodshed than the suppression of the risings of slaves, serfs or wage laborers, and it will cost mankind far less. And it is compatible with the extension of democracy to such an overwhelming majority of the population that the need for a *special machine* of suppression will begin to disappear. The exploiters are naturally unable to suppress the people without a highly complex machine for performing this task; but *the people* can suppress the exploiters even with a very simple "machine," almost without a "machine," without a special apparatus, but the simple *organization of the armed masses* (such as the Soviets of Workers' and Soldiers' Deputies, let us remark, anticipating somewhat).

THE CRISIS HAS MATURED

Although Lenin's enforced absence from public leadership of the party restricted his influence on its policy, he contrived by messages, articles, and, at the end, participation in secret meetings to push the Bolsheviks toward a gamble for power. Earlier in 1917 Lenin himself had considered a Bolshevik *coup* too risky, but by October he was so convinced that the strategic moment had arrived that he was willing to go to almost any lengths to have his way. When the Central Committee was hesitant in accepting his demand for an uprising, he even submitted his resignation—in gross violation of the standard of party discipline that he applied to others.

In a literal sense the Committee called his bluff, for no *coup* was attempted for some weeks after the submission on September 29 [October 12 New Style] of the letter from which the following excerpt is taken. And Lenin did not actually resign from the Central Committee; he preferred, instead, to continue his exhortations to action. Nor did the delay prove as dangerous as he had predicted, for the October Revolution (November, New Style) succeeded even though it almost coincided with the opening of the Second All-Russian Congress of Soviets, contrary to Lenin's wishes.

In a larger sense, however, Lenin had correctly divined that his best chance for seizing power had arrived, and he had correctly predicted the comparative strength of the opposing forces.

The first portion of the following material, as Lenin's own instructions indicate, was intended for publication, and it appeared on October 7 [October 20, New Style] in *Rabochii i Soldat* (*The Worker and Soldier*). But the latter part, including the threat of resignation, was intended only for limited circulation and was published only in 1925. Angry as he really was with his followers, Lenin was too shrewd to make public his statement on resignation, which would have restricted his own maneuverability while making it more difficult for his Bolshevik opponents to retreat.

It is impossible to doubt it. We stand on the threshold of international proletarian revolution. And since we—the Russian Bolsheviks—alone

From "The Crisis Has Matured." Lenin, *Sochineniia*, 3rd ed. (Moscow, 1928), XXI, 235-241. Editor's translation.

among the proletarian internationalists of all countries, enjoy comparatively broad freedom, have an above-ground party, have a score or so newspapers, have on our side the Soviets of Workers' and Soldiers' Deputies in the capitals [Petrograd and Moscow—*ed.*], have on our side *the majority* of the masses of the people at a revolutionary time, then we may and must apply to ourselves the dictum: much is asked of him to whom much is given. . . .

The crisis has matured. The whole future of the Russian Revolution is at stake. The whole honor of the Bolshevik Party is at issue. The whole future of the international workers' revolution for socialism is at stake.

The crisis has matured . . . [Ellipsis Lenin's—*ed.*]

———

The foregoing may be published, but the following is for *distribution to members of the Central Committee, Petrograd Committee, Moscow Committee, and the Soviets.*

———

What, then, is to be done? We must *aussprechen was ist,* "say what is," recognize the truth that in our Central Committee, in the high levels of our party, there is a tendency or an opinion in favor of *waiting* for the Congress of Soviets, *against* the rapid seizure of power, *against* a rapid uprising. It is necessary to *overcome* this tendency or opinion.

Otherwise the Bolsheviks will be *shamed* forever and *will become a nullity* as a party.

For to miss such a moment and "wait" for the Congress of Soviets is *utter idiocy* or *utter betrayal. . . .*

To "wait" for the Congress of Soviets is utter idiocy, for this means we will waste a week, but a week and even days now determine *everything.* It signifies the cowardly *renunciation* of the seizure of power, because on November 1-2 [November 14-15, New Style] it will be impossible (both politically and technically: they will muster the Cossacks against the day of the foolishly "appointed" uprising).

To "wait" for the Congress of Soviets is utter idiocy, for the Congress *will give nothing, can give nothing.*

The "moral" significance? Astounding! The "significance" of resolutions and discussions with the Liberdans [a composite of the names of two moderate socialist leaders—*ed.*] when we know that the Soviets are *for* the peasants and that they [the Liberdans—*ed.*] *are suppressing* the peasant uprising. Thus we will reduce the Soviets to the role of miserable chatterers. First defeat Kerensky, then call the Congress.

The victory of the uprising is now *secure* for the Bolsheviks: (1) we can (if we do not "wait" for the Congress of Soviets) attack *suddenly* from three points, from Peter [Petrograd—*ed.*], from Moscow, from the Baltic fleet; (2) we have slogans for which support is guaranteed: Down with the government that suppresses the peasant uprising against the landlords!

(3) We have a majority in the *country;* (4) the collapse of the Mensheviks and SR's is complete; (5) we have the technical means of seizing power in Moscow (which might even be the place to start in order to take the enemy by surprise); (6) we have *thousands* of armed workers and soldiers in Peter, who can *at once* seize the Winter Palace, the General Staff Building, the telephone exchange, and all the major printing shops; they will not dislodge us from these places, and the agitation in the *army* will become such that it will be *impossible* to fight against this government of peace, of peasants' land, etc.

If we attack at once, suddenly, from the three points, Peter, Moscow, and the Baltic fleet, then the chances are ninety-nine out of one hundred that we will win with fewer casualties than on July 3-5 [July 16-18, New Style] because *the troops will not come out* against a government of peace. Even if Kerensky *already* has "loyal" cavalry and so on in Peter, when we strike on two sides and have the sympathy of the army *with us,* Kerensky will be obliged *to surrender.* If, with such chances as the present ones, we do not seize power, then all the talk about power to the Soviets becomes a *lie.*

Not to take power now, to "wait," to chatter in the Central Executive Committee [of the Petrograd Soviet—*ed.*], to limit oneself to "the struggle for the organ" (of the Soviet), "the struggle for the congress," signifies *the ruin of the revolution.*

Seeing that the Central Committee leaves my urgings along these lines *without even an answer,* that the Central Organ [the newspaper—*ed.*] *deletes* from my articles references to such glaring errors of the Bolsheviks as the shameful decision to participate in the preparliament [an assembly convened by the Provisional Government—*ed.*], as the allocation to the Mensheviks of seats on the presidium of the Soviets, etc., etc., seeing all this, I am obliged to recognize here a "gentle" hint that the Central Committee does not even wish to consider this question, a gentle hint at gagging me and a suggestion that I withdraw.

I am obliged *to submit my resignation to the Central Committee,* which I hereby do, retaining my freedom to agitate *in the lower ranks* of the party and at the party congress.

For it is my profoundest conviction that if we "wait" for the Congress of Soviets and miss the present moment, we *ruin* the revolution.

TO THE WORKERS, SOLDIERS,
AND PEASANTS

Just as the Bolsheviks, operating through the Military Revolution-ary Committee of the Petrograd Soviet, were completing their seizure of the key centers in the capital on the night of October 25 [November 7, New Style] the Second All-Russian Congress of Soviets convened. Contrary to Lenin's gloomy expectations concerning this body, it contained a majority of pro-Bolsheviks (including Left Socialist Revolutionaries), and soon after it opened was converted into a wholly pro-Bolshevik body, as the Menshevik and Socialist Revolutionary opponents of the *coup d'état* demonstratively withdrew.

Trotsky was the main Bolshevik spokesman at the first meeting of the Congress, for Lenin cautiously refrained from appearing before the meeting until the night of October 26 [November 8, New Style], when he presented his important decrees on peace and land. But Lenin did use the first session of the Congress as a tribune from which to proclaim the general outlines of the policy of the new government—of which Lenin was not yet a member, technically. A. V. Lunacharsky, a second-rank Bolshevik, read to the Congress the following manifesto, which Lenin had composed and which sketched the main policies of his regime. It was published in *Rabochii i Soldat* on October 26 [November 8, New Style].

Since Lenin's immediate concern was political survival, the proclamation is of interest as an appeal to public opinion rather than as a blueprint for Soviet Russia. Faced by a counterattack by Kerensky—which Lenin somewhat overrated—and the task of gaining at least the passive support of the masses of the populace—which could hardly be overrated as a challenge—Lenin was bound to be quite free with optimistic promises.

The Second All-Russian Congress of Soviets of Workers' and Soldiers' Deputies has opened. The vast majority of the Soviets are represented at the Congress. A number of delegates from the Peasants' Soviets are also present. The mandate of the compromising Central Executive Committee

From "To the Workers, Soldiers, and Peasants." Lenin, *Selected Works*, Vol. II, Part I, 327-28.

has terminated. Backed by the will of the vast majority of the workers, soldiers and peasants, backed by the victorious uprising of the workers and the garrison which has taken place in Petrograd, the Congress takes the power into its own hands.

The Provisional Government has been overthrown. The majority of the members of the Provisional Government have already been arrested.

The Soviet government will propose an immediate democratic peace to all the nations and an immediate armistice on all fronts. It will secure the transfer of the land of the landlords, of the crown and monasteries to the peasants' committees without compensation; it will protect the rights of the soldiers by introducing complete democracy in the army; it will establish workers' control over production; it will ensure the convocation of the Constituent Assembly at the time appointed; it will see to it that bread is supplied to the cities and prime necessities to the villages; it will guarantee all the nations inhabiting Russia the genuine right of self-determination.

The Congress decrees: all power in the localities shall pass to the Soviets of Workers', Soldiers' and Peasants' Deputies, which must guarantee genuine revolutionary order.

The Congress calls upon the soldiers in the trenches to be vigilant and firm. The Congress of Soviets is convinced that the revolutionary army will be able to defend the revolution against all attacks of imperialism until such time as the new government succeeds in concluding a democratic peace, which it will propose directly to all peoples. The new government will do everything to supply all the needs of the revolutionary army by means of a determined policy of requisitions and taxation of the propertied classes, and also will improve the condition of soldiers' families.

The Kornilovites—Kerensky, Kaledin ["counterrevolutionary" leaders—*ed.*] and others—are attempting to bring troops against Petrograd. Several detachments, whom Kerensky had got to move by deceit, have come over to the side of the insurgent people.

Soldiers, actively resist Kerensky, the Kornilovite! Be on your guard!

Railwaymen, hold up all troop trains dispatched by Kerensky against Petrograd!

Soldiers, workers and employees, the fate of the revolution and the fate of the democratic peace is in your hands!

Long live the Revolution!

DRAFT DECREE ON THE
DISSOLUTION OF THE
CONSTITUENT ASSEMBLY

Although Lenin regarded the party—or himself—as the true guardian of the interests of the masses, he could not ignore the challenge presented by the Russian Constituent Assembly, which was elected by broadly democratic suffrage in November, 1917, and convened in Moscow on January 18, 1918. Not only did this body have a much greater claim to representative legitimacy than did the Congress of Soviets or the Bolshevik Central Committee, it had been repeatedly, earlier in the year, called for by Lenin and his followers. True, they had insisted on the convocation of the Constituent Assembly mainly to embarrass the Provisional Government, but this, joined to the recognition accorded the assembly by all other parties, still helped to make it formidable in prestige when it at last appeared.

The elections showed that the Bolsheviks had far outstripped the liberal parties and the Mensheviks in popular appeal, but the Socialist Revolutionary Party, the one best known among the peasantry, came into the conference with a plurality in popular votes and—under the mechanism of the Assembly—an absolute majority of deputies. Even though a substantial group of Left Socialist Revolutionaries supported the Bolsheviks, the Assembly had not been in session many hours before it was apparent that the Bolsheviks would have to yield political primacy to their opponents in the Assembly or dissolve it. Lenin readily chose the latter course, and in the following document attempted to rationalize—on the basis of Marxist assumptions—his use of force to disperse the meeting on January 19. The event was important not only in the politics of the Russian revolution but also in the life of European socialism, for Lenin's dictatorial measures incurred the criticism of various leaders of the western Marxist parties, deepening the rift in the international movement.

At its very inception, the Russian revolution gave rise to Soviets of Workers', Soldiers' and Peasants' Deputies as the only mass organization of all the toiling and exploited classes capable of leading the struggle of these classes for their complete political and economic emancipation.

During the whole of the initial period of the Russian revolution the Soviets multiplied in number, grew and gained strength, were taught by their own experience to discard the illusions of compromise with the bourgeoisie and to realize the deceptive nature of the forms of bourgeois-democratic parliamentarism, and arrived by practical experience at the conclusion that the emancipation of the oppressed classes was impossible unless they broke with these forms and with every kind of compromise. Such a break was the October Revolution, which transferred the entire power to the Soviets.

The Constituent Assembly, elected on the basis of lists drawn up prior to the October Revolution, was an expression of the old relation of political forces which existed when power was held by the compromisers and the Kadets. When the people at that time voted for the candidates of the Socialist Revolutionary Party, they were not in a position to choose between the Right Socialist Revolutionaries, the supporters of the bourgeoisie, and the Left Socialist Revolutionaries, the supporters of socialism. Thus the Constituent Assembly, which was to have been the crown of the bourgeois parliamentary republic, could not but become an obstacle in the path of the October Revolution and the Soviet power.

The October Revolution, by giving the power to the Soviets, and through the Soviets to the toiling and exploited classes, aroused the desperate resistance of the exploiters, and in the crushing of this resistance it fully revealed itself as the beginning of the socialist revolution. The toiling classes learnt by experience that the old bourgeois parliamentarism had outlived its purpose and was absolutely incompatible with the aim of achieving socialism, and that not national institutions, but only class institutions (such as the Soviets), were capable of overcoming the resistance of the propertied classes and of laying the foundations of a socialist society. To relinquish the sovereign power of the Soviets, to relinquish the Soviet republic won by the people, for the sake of bourgeois parliamentarism and the Constituent Assembly, would now be a retrograde step and cause the collapse of the October workers' and peasants' revolution.

Owing to the circumstances mentioned above, the majority in the Constituent Assembly which met on January 5 was secured by the party of the Right Socialist Revolutionaries, the party of Kerensky, Avksentiev and Chernov. Naturally, this party refused to discuss the absolutely clear, precise and unambiguous proposal of the supreme organ of Soviet power, the Central Executive Committee of the Soviets, to recognize the program of the Soviet power, to recognize the "Declaration of Rights of the Toiling and Exploited People," to recognize the October Revolution and the Soviet power. Thereby the Constituent Assembly severed all ties with the Soviet Republic of Russia. The withdrawal from such a Constituent Assembly of the Groups of the Bolsheviks and the Left Socialist Revolutionaries, who now patently constitute the overwhelming majority in the Soviets and enjoy the confidence of the workers and the majority of the peasants, was inevitable.

The Right Socialist Revolutionary and Menshevik parties are in fact waging outside the walls of the Constituent Assembly a most desperate struggle against the Soviet power, calling openly in their press for its overthrow and characterizing as arbitrary and unlawful the crushing by force of the resistance of the exploiters by the toiling classes, which is essential in the interests of emancipation from exploitation. They are defending the saboteurs, the servitors of capital, and are going to the length of undisguised calls to terrorism, which certain "unidentified groups" have already begun to practise. It is obvious that under such circumstances the remaining part of the Constituent Assembly could only serve as a screen for the struggle of the counterrevolutionaries to overthrow the Soviet power.

Accordingly, the Central Executive Committee [of the Congress of Soviets—*ed.*] resolves:

The Constituent Assembly is hereby dissolved.

THE PROLETARIAN REVOLUTION
AND THE RENEGADE KAUTSKY

Despite the preoccupations of directing the government of a large state during a time of crisis, Lenin's combative character did not permit him to relax the scope or the intensity of his polemical literary activity. Perhaps the prime postrevolutionary example of his pamphleteering is the work from which the following excerpt is drawn, the very title of which breathes self-righteousness and contempt. In this pronouncement as in others from the same period, Lenin demonstrated how he regarded the First World War and the Bolshevik Revolution as the crucial events of the century, the former because it demolished a phase and a species of socialism, the latter because it opened a new phase. According to Lenin, the "rotten" socialism that he had castigated throughout the war ("European" socialism he calls it in contemptuous quotation marks) had yielded to the truly revolutionary socialism that had achieved its finest flowering in Russia (and in Lenin, one may gather). This, he argued, must be reflected in the formation of a new, militant Marxist International, a goal that he established in his "April (1917) Theses" and that he began to realize in the First and Second Congresses of the Third or Communist International (Comintern in contraction) in March, 1919, and August, 1920.

The immediate occasion of this composition of October-November, 1918 was the appearance of a pamphlet entitled "The Dictatorship of the Proletariat" by Karl Kautsky, the German Social Democrat. Lenin's counterattack was exceptionally virulent, partly because of his usual feelings about the "social-patriots" who had "betrayed" the proletariat and partly because Kautsky's critique touched a very sensitive spot. Although the completion of the Bolshevik totalitarian machine was still some years away, all rival political parties had been suppressed and the population had been deprived of any significant means of expressing itself through ballots. The Leninist claim to legitimacy rested on the postulate that the Bolsheviks represented the masses and that the other parties, including the rival Socialist parties, were "bourgeois." Since Lenin could not afford to submit this claim to any objective test, it is not surprising that he found harsh epithets all the more necessary.

At the time of the composition of this article the prospects for revolution in the West never seemed better. The pamphlet was written just as the World War ground to its end and the German and Austro-Hungarian Empires collapsed. In Germany the extreme left, led by Karl Liebknecht and Rosa Luxemburg, was gaining ground rapidly, and workers and military personnel seemed disposed toward revolution. Only in January, 1919, did this movement receive a severe check with the collapse of a premature uprising. It was quite reasonable for Lenin to believe in October-November, 1918, that the Russian revolution was but the first explosion of a series and that the Soviet state would soon have the assistance of socialist governments in the more highly industrialized countries.

Let the contemptible scoundrelly renegades, amidst the applause of the bourgeoisie and the social-chauvinists, abuse our Soviet Constitution for disfranchising the exploiters! That is well, because it will accelerate and widen the split between the revolutionary workers of Europe and the Scheidemanns and Kautskys, the Renaudels and Longuets, the Hendersons and Ramsay MacDonalds, the old leaders and old betrayers of socialism.

The masses of the oppressed classes, the class-conscious and honest revolutionary proletarian leaders, will be on *our side*. It will be sufficient to acquaint such proletarians and such masses with our Soviet Constitution for them to say at once: "These are really *our people*, this is a real workers' party, this is a real workers' government; for it does not deceive the workers by talking about reforms in the way *all the above-mentioned leaders have done*, but is fighting the exploiters in real earnest, is making a revolution in real earnest and is *actually* fighting for the complete emancipation of the workers."

The *fact* that after a year's "experience" the Soviets have deprived the exploiters of the franchise *shows* that the Soviets are really organizations of the oppressed masses and not of social-imperialists and social-pacifists who have sold themselves to the bourgeoisie. The *fact* that the Soviets have disfranchised the exploiters *shows* that they are not organs of petty-bourgeois compromise with the capitalists, not organs of parliamentary chatter (on the part of the Kautskys, the Longuets and the MacDonalds), but organs of the genuinely revolutionary proletariat which is waging a life and death struggle against the exploiters.

"Kautsky's book is almost unknown here," a well-informed comrade in Berlin wrote to me a few days ago (today is October 30). I would advise our ambassadors in Germany and Switzerland not to stint thousands in buying up this book and *distributing it gratis* among the

class-conscious workers in order to trample in the mud this "European"
—read: imperialist and reformist—Social Democracy, which has long
been a "stinking corpse."

At the end of his book, on pages 61 and 63, Mr. Kautsky bitterly
laments the fact that the "new theory" (as he calls Bolshevism, fearing
even to touch Marx's and Engels' analysis of the Paris Commune) "finds
supporters even in old democracies like Switzerland, for instance." "It
is incomprehensible" to Kautsky "how this theory can be adopted by
German Social Democrats."

No, it is quite comprehensible; for after the serious lessons of the war
the revolutionary masses are becoming sick and tired of the Scheidemanns and the Kautskys.

"We" have always been in favour of democracy, Kautsky writes, yet
we are supposed suddenly to renounce it!

"We," the opportunists of Social Democracy, have always been opposed to the dictatorship of the proletariat, and Kolbs and Co. proclaimed this *long ago*. Kautsky knows this and vainly expects that he
will be able to conceal from his readers the obvious fact that he has
"returned to the fold" of the Bernsteins and Kolbs [German "revisionist" Marxists—*ed.*].

"We," the revolutionary Marxists, have never made a fetish of "pure"
(bourgeois) democracy. As is known, in 1903 Plekhanov was a revolutionary Marxist (before his unfortunate turn, which brought him to the
position of a Russian Schiedemann). And in that year Plekhanov declared at the congress of our Party, which was then adopting its program, that in the revolution the proletariat would, if necessary, disfran-
chise the capitalists and *disperse any parliament* that was found to be
counterrevolutionary. That this is the only view that corresponds to
Marxism will be clear to anybody even from the statements of Marx and
Engels which I have quoted above; it follows obviously from all the fundamental principles of Marxism.

"We," the revolutionary Marxists, never made the speeches to the
people that the Kautskyites of all nations love to make, cringing before
the bourgeoisie, adapting themselves to bourgeois parliamentarism, keeping silent about the *bourgeois* character of modern democracy and demanding only *its* extension, only that *it* be carried to its logical conclusion.

"We" said to the bourgeoisie: You, exploiters and hypocrites, talk
about democracy, while at every step you erect thousands of barriers to
prevent the *oppressed masses* from taking part in politics. We take you at
your word and, in the interests of these masses, demand the extension of
your bourgeois democracy *in order to prepare the masses for revolution*
for the purpose of overthrowing you, the exploiters. And if you exploiters

attempt to offer resistance to our proletarian revolution we will ruthlessly suppress you; we will deprive you of all rights; more than that, we
will not give you any bread, for in our proletarian republic the exploiters will have no rights, they will be deprived of fire and water, for
we are Socialists in real earnest and not in the Scheidemann, Kautsky
fashion.

That is what "we," the revolutionary Marxists, said, and will say—
and that is why the oppressed masses will support us and be with us,
while the Scheidemanns and Kautskys will be swept into the renegade's
cesspool. . . .

The Bolsheviks' tactics were correct; they were the *only* internationalist tactics, because they were based, not on the cowardly fear of a world
revolution, not on a philistine "lack of faith" in it, not on the narrow
nationalist desire to protect one's "own" fatherland (the fatherland of
one's own bourgeoisie), while not "caring a hang" about all the rest,
but on a correct (and, before the war and before the apostasy of the
social-chauvinists and social-pacifists, a universally admitted) *estimation*
of the revolutionary situation in Europe. These tactics were the only
internationalist tactics, because they did the utmost possible in one country *for* the development, support and awakening of the revolution in *all
countries*. These tactics have been justified by their enormous success,
for bolshevism (not by any means because of the merits of the Russian
Bolsheviks, but because of the most profound sympathy of the *masses*
everywhere for tactics that are revolutionary in practice) has become
world bolshevism, has produced an idea, a theory, a program and tactics, which differ concretely and in practice from those of social-chauvin-
ism and social-pacifism. Bolshevism *has given a coup de grâce* to the old,
decayed International of the Scheidemanns and Kautskys, Renaudels and
Longuets, Hendersons and the MacDonalds, who henceforth will be
treading on each other's heels, dreaming about "unity" and trying to
revive a corpse. Bolshevism has *created* the ideological and tactical foundations of a Third International, of a really proletarian and Communist
International, which will take into consideration both the gains of the
epoch of peace and the experience of the *epoch of revolutions, which
has begun*.

Bolshevism has popularized throughout the world the idea of the
"dictatorship of the proletariat," has translated these words from the
Latin, first into Russian, and then into *all* the languages of the world,
and has shown by the example of the *Soviet power* that the workers and
poor peasants, *even* of a backward country, even with the least experience, education and habits of organization, *have been able* for a whole
year, amidst gigantic difficulties and amidst a struggle against the exploiters (who were supported by the bourgeoisie of the *whole* world)
to maintain the power of the toilers, to create a democracy that is im-

measurably higher and broader than all previous democracies in the world, and to *start* the creative work of tens of millions of workers and peasants for the practical achievement of socialism.

Bolshevism has actually helped to develop the proletarian revolution in Europe and America more powerfully than any party in any other country has so far succeeded in doing. While the workers of the whole world are realizing more and more clearly every day that the tactics of the Scheidemanns and Kautskys have not delivered them from the imperialist war and from wage-slavery to the imperialist bourgeoisie, and that these tactics cannot serve as a model for all countries, the masses of the proletarians of all countries are realizing more and more clearly every day that bolshevism has indicated the right road of escape from the horrors of war and imperialism, that bolshevism *can serve as a model of tactics for all.*

Not only the general European but the world proletarian revolution is maturing before the eyes of all, and it has been assisted, accelerated and supported by the victory of the proletariat in Russia. All this is not enough for the complete victory of socialism, you say? Of course it is not enough. One country alone cannot do more. But this one country, thanks to the Soviet power, has done so much that even if the Soviet power in Russia were to be crushed by world imperialism tomorrow, as a result, let us say, of an agreement between German and Anglo-French imperialism—even granted that very worst possibility—it would still be found that Bolshevik tactics have brought enormous benefit to socialism and have assisted the growth of the invincible world revolution.

LENIN ON THE INDUSTRIALIZATION
OF RUSSIA

The world revolution that Lenin had expected did not materialize, and circumstances required that he do what was possible to
advance toward the ideal society in Russia alone. Since he did not
live long enough to give up hope that world revolution was imminent, he did not develop any general theory about the possibility of building socialism in a single country, as Stalin was soon
to do. Nevertheless, Lenin placed great emphasis on the importance
of modernizing the Russian economy under the direction of a
central planning agency. In the short run, economic advance was
obviously necessary to provide for the defence of the Soviet state,
but Lenin also noted that the long-term importance of this development was the provision of the economic basis for a socialist
society. Since Lenin seemed to believe that this basis could be
provided by Russia's own resources, with no assistance from friendly,
"proletarian" revolutions abroad, one might well conclude Lenin
was about ready to admit that Russia might build "socialism in
one country."

Evidently Lenin's optimism concerning Russia's economic development leaned heavily on the presumed advantages of stressing
the most modern of all technical development: the electrical field.
So great was his enthusiasm for his solution to the basic economic
problems of the country that he described the first plan for Goelro
(State Commission for the Electrification of Russia) as a "second
party program." His remarks on this development at the Eighth
All-Russian Congress of Soviets in December, 1920, illustrate well
the trend of his thought on the future of Soviet Russia and its
economy. Although no great improvement in the capacity of
Soviet industry or agriculture resulted directly from Goelro, the
project was of real practical importance as an early experiment in
state-directed economic development. And its mythological importance in the cult of Lenin, as developed immediately after the
leader's death in 1924, is greater still.

Communism is Soviet power plus the electrification of the whole country. Otherwise the country remains small-peasant, as we are bound to recognize. We are weaker than capitalism, not only on a world scale but also within the country. All this is well-known. We recognize this and we are taking action to transform the small-peasant base into a heavy-industry base. Only when the country is electrified, when industry, agriculture, and transport are placed on the technical basis of modern heavy industry, will we have won decisively.

Already we have worked out a preliminary plan for the electrification of the country, a plan on which two hundred of our best scientific and technical forces have worked. The plan that has been worked out provides us with a material and financial estimate for a long period, not less than ten years. This plan states how many million buckets of cement and how many million bricks we need to introduce electrification. In financial terms the introduction of electrification is estimated at 1-1.2 million gold rubles. You know that our gold supply is far from enough to cover this whole sum. And our food supply, also, is not great. Therefore we must cover these estimates with concessions by this plan, of which I have spoken. You will note that it is on this basis that it is planned to reconstruct our industry and transport.

Not long ago I was at a peasant celebration in an outlying area of Moscow province, Volokamsky district, where the peasants have electric lighting. They held a meeting on the street and there one of the peasants gave a speech in which he welcomed this new event in the life of the peasants. He said that we, the peasants, were in darkness and now light appears to us, "unnatural light that will illuminate our peasant darkness." I was not surprised by these words. Of course for the nonparty peasant masses electric light is "unnatural" light, but for us it is unnatural that for hundreds, thousands of years peasants and workers could live in such darkness, in poverty, under the oppression of landlords and capitalists. From this darkness they will not quickly emerge. But at present we must make it our goal that every electric plant we build becomes a support for enlightenment, that it is devoted, so to speak, to the electrical education of the masses. We have worked out a plan for electrification, but the fulfillment of this plan is reckoned in years. Whatever happens, we must realize this plan and reduce the term of its fulfillment. In this, we should do as we have done with one of our first economic plans, the one for the reestablishment of transport—order No. 1042—which was calculated as five years, which is fulfillment beyond the norm.

But one must know and remember that the introduction of electrification cannot be while we have illiteracy. It is not enough that our com-

"Lenin on the Industrialization of Russia." From: "Report on the Activities of the Council of People's Commissars." Lenin, *Sochineniia*, XXVI, 24-59. Editor's translation.

mission will struggle to liquidate illiteracy. It has done much in comparison with the former situation but little in comparison with what is needed. In addition to literacy, cultured, conscientious, educated workers are needed; the majority of the peasants must set before themselves the tasks that we have before us. This program of the party [a book on Goelro—*ed.*] should become a basic book which should be introduced into all schools. You have in it a series of general plans for the introduction of electrification, special plans for each region of Russia. And each comrade who goes into a locality will have a definite elaboration of the introduction of electrification into his region, the transition from darkness to normal existence. And comrades, you can and must in each locality compare, elaborate, and verify the data of your situation, with this objective: that whenever in any school, any circle, they answer the question, "what is communism?" they will answer not only what is written in the party program but they will speak also of the emergence from the state of darkness. . . .

We must strive, that each factory, each electrical power plant becomes a hearth of enlightenment; if Russia is covered with a thick network of electric stations and powerful technical equipment, then our communistic economic structure will become a model for the coming socialist Europe and Asia.

ON THE UNITY OF THE PARTY

Although unity and discipline in the party had been a continuous precept of Leninism ever since the publication of "What Is to Be Done?" in 1902, the reaffirmation and elaboration of this point in March, 1921, was an event of considerable significance. It is perhaps the most important doctrinal link between the prerevolutionary idea of the party and Soviet-era bolshevism, leading eventually to full-blown Stalinism. Before 1917 Lenin sometimes excused the stringency of Bolshevik discipline by citing the peculiarly difficult conditions imposed by tsardom, and it might have been argued, especially *after* the crisis of the Russian Civil War, that the Bolshevik victory made possible a less monolithic order in the party. In his resolution "On the Unity of the Party," however, Lenin disavowed any such idea, maintaining in effect that the continuing class struggle in and around Russia still precluded even moderate pluralism in the party.

This not only stifled the comparatively minor heresies of the day, chiefly the "Workers' Opposition" (certain Bolsheviks who favored a degree of trade-union autonomy), but foreshadowed the years of repressions that lay ahead. The seventh point, empowering the Central Committee to expel heretics, provides a particularly interesting illustration of the continuity from Lenin to Stalin. Lenin emphatically favored this authoritarian manifesto, a natural corollary of so much of his reasoning, but he evidently felt some embarrassment over its bluntness and abstained from having it published with the rest of resolution in 1921. Only in 1924 did Stalin make public this part of the resolution, an excellent weapon against his rivals for power following Lenin's death. Where Lenin had been able to achieve the substance of his intended suppression of dissidence, just short of a frank threat, Stalin could not afford such diplomacy and unveiled the harsh warning. But the difference between the men was in circumstance and style, not in principle.

In the background of the Tenth Party Congress, which adopted the gist of Lenin's resolution on unity, lay the still-smoldering revolt of the prorevolutionary sailors of the Kronstadt naval fortress, not far from Leningrad. This armed upheaval was directed not against socialism but against Bolshevik dictatorship, and Lenin could hardly have welcomed it. But it undoubtedly helped to provide a pretext for the adoption of this rigorous resolution, an emergency that has been in force ever since.

1. The Congress calls the attention of all members of the party to the fact that the unity and solidarity of the ranks of the party, ensuring complete mutual confidence among party members, and genuine team work, genuinely embodying the unanimity of will of the vanguard of the proletariat, are particularly essential at the present juncture when a number of circumstances are increasing the vacillation among the petty-bourgeois population of the country.

2. Notwithstanding this, even before the general party discussion on the trade unions, certain signs of factionalism had been apparent in the party, viz., the formation of groups with separate platforms, striving to a certain degree to segregate and create their own group discipline. Such symptoms of factionalism were manifested, for example, at a party conference in Moscow (November 1920) and in Kharkov, both by the so-called "Workers' Opposition" group, and partly by the so-called "Democratic-Centralism" group.

All class-conscious workers must clearly realize the perniciousness and impermissibility of factionalism of any kind, for no matter how the representatives of individual groups may desire to safeguard party unity, in practice factionalism inevitably leads to the weakening of team work and to intensified and repeated attempts by the enemies of the party, who have fastened themselves onto it because it is the governing party, to widen the cleavage and to use it for counterrevolutionary purposes.

The way the enemies of the proletariat take advantage of every deviation from the thoroughly consistent Communist line was perhaps most strikingly shown in the case of the Kronstadt mutiny, when the bourgeois counterrevolutionaries and Whiteguards in all countries of the world immediately expressed their readiness to accept even the slogans of the Soviet system, if only they might thereby secure the overthrow of the dictatorship of the proletariat in Russia, and [when] the bourgeois counterrevolutionaries in general resorted in Kronstadt to slogans calling for an insurrection against the Soviet government ostensibly in the interest of Soviet power. These facts fully prove that the Whiteguards strive, and are able, to disguise themselves as Communists and even as the most Left Communists, solely for the purpose of weakening and overthrowing the bulwark of the proletarian revolution in Russia. Menshevik leaflets distributed in Petrograd on the eve of the Kronstadt mutiny likewise show how the Mensheviks took advantage of the disagreements and certain rudimentary factionalism in the Russian Communist Party actually in order to egg on and support the Kronstadt mutineers, the Socialist Revolutionaries and Whiteguards, while claiming to be opponents of mutiny and supporters of the Soviet power, only with supposedly slight modification.

3. In this question propaganda should consist, on the one hand, of a comprehensive explanation of the harmfulness and danger of fac-

tionalism from the point of view of party unity and of achieving unanimity of will among the vanguard of the proletariat as the fundamental condition for the success of the dictatorship of the proletariat; and, on the other hand, of an explanation of the peculiar features of the latest tactical devices of the enemies of Soviet power. These enemies, having realized the hopelessness of counterrevolution under an openly White-guard flag, are now doing their utmost to utilize the disagreements within the Russian Communist Party and to further the counterrevolution in one way or another by transferring power to the political groupings which outwardly are closest to the recognition of Soviet power. . . .

4. In the practical struggle against factionalism, every organization of the party must take strict measures to prevent any factional actions whatsoever. Criticism of the party's shortcomings, which is absolutely necessary, must be conducted in such a way that every practical proposal shall be submitted immediately, without any delay, in the most precise form possible, for consideration and decision to the leading local and central bodies of the party. Moreover, everyone who criticizes must see to it that the form of his criticism takes into account the position of the party, surrounded as it is by a ring of enemies, and that the content of his criticism is such that, by directly participating in Soviet and party work, he can test the rectification of the errors of the party or of individual party members in practice. Every analysis of the general line of the party, estimate of the practical experience, verification of the fulfillment of decisions, study of methods of rectifying error, etc., must under no circumstances be submitted for preliminary discussion to groups formed on the basis of "platforms," etc., but must be exclusively submitted for discussion directly to all members of the party. . . .

5. Rejecting in principle the deviations toward syndicalism and anarchism, to the examination of which a separate resolution is devoted, and instructing the Central Committee to secure the complete elimination of all factionalism, the Congress at the same time declares that every practical proposal concerning questions to which the so-called Workers' Opposition group, for example, has devoted special attention, such as purging the party of nonproletarian and unreliable elements, combating bureaucracy, developing democracy and the initiative of workers, etc., must be examined with the greatest care and tried out in practical work. The party must know that we do not take all the measures that are necessary in regard to these questions, because we encounter a number of obstacles of various kinds, and [party members must know] that, while ruthlessly rejecting impractical and factional pseudo-criticisms, the party will unceasingly continue—trying out new methods—to fight with all the means at its disposal against bureaucracy, for the extension of democracy and initiative, for detecting, exposing and expelling from the party [those] elements that have wormed their way into its ranks, etc.

6. The Congress therefore hereby declares dissolved and orders the immediate dissolution of all groups without exception that have been formed on the basis of one platform or another (such as the "Workers' Opposition" group, the "Democratic Centralism" group, etc.). Nonobservance of this decision of the Congress shall involve absolute and immediate expulsion from the party.

7. In order to ensure strict discipline within the party and in all Soviet work and to secure the maximum unanimity in removing all factionalism, the Congress authorizes the Central Committee, in cases of breach of discipline or of a revival or toleration of factionalism, to apply all party penalties, including expulsion, and in regard to members of the Central Committee to reduce them to the status of alternate members, and even, as an extreme measure to expel them from the party. A necessary condition for the application of such an extreme measure to members of the Central Committee, alternate members of the Central Committee and members of the Control Commission is the convocation of a plenum of the Central Committee, to which all alternate members of the Central Committee and all members of the Control Commission shall be invited. If such a general assembly of the most responsible leaders of the party, by a two-thirds majority, deems it necessary to reduce a member of the Central Committee to the status of alternate member, or to expel him from the Party, this measure shall be put into effect immediately.

LENIN'S TESTAMENT

In May, 1922, Lenin suffered the first of the cerebral hemorrhages that finally ended his life in January, 1924. The first stroke was not too severe, and Lenin began to resume limited activity the latter part of the summer of 1922. Perhaps the enforced leisure improved Lenin's perspective on the evolution of Bolshevik-dominated Russia, for he soon began to detect what he considered to be dangerous tendencies in the highest circles. The most general, basic criticism that Lenin developed was of the growing tendency toward "bureaucratism," a widening gulf between the leading circles and the masses. He had long approved of dictatorship directed against the opponents of Bolshevik "truth"; but it seemed that a dictatorship not *of* but *over* the proletariat was emerging. More specifically, Lenin came to see Joseph Stalin as the chief representative of the new tendency. Stalin, thanks to Lenin's personal support, had acquired numerous important posts in the hierarchy of the party. Of these, the office of General Secretary was the most powerful, controlling the appointment of thousands of Communist officials. Lenin felt special annoyance at Stalin for his rough treatment of some Georgian Communists who differed with the policy of the central organs of the party.

All of Lenin's criticism contained an element of self-reproach, for it was he who had established the principles of centralism and iron discipline in the name of a proletariat that was never really consulted. It was Lenin who had presided over the growth of a large bureaucracy, having found that it was impossible to transfer political power directly into the hands of the ordinary populace, as he had envisioned in "State and Revolution." And it was Lenin who had recognized the administrative ability and willpower of the rather drab Stalin.

Between recurrences of his illness, Lenin grappled with the question of reforming his own creation, but it does not appear that he ever reached a definite conclusion. One sort of "solution" that he considered in late 1922 and early 1923 reflected his utopian side. Harking back to the ideas of "State and Revolution," he proposed various schemes by which ordinary workers would audit the work of the party officials, having access to all important state papers. A less lofty, morally optimistic approach was to remove the offending bureaucrats, which Lenin privately recommended in the case of Stalin. But he could not bring himself to implement this latter proposal while his health held up, and no one else was capable of removing Stalin subsequently.

The most important document from this anguished period in Lenin's life is usually known as his "Testament" although he simply considered it part of a "letter" or "memorandum" addressed to the Twelfth Party Congress, which was scheduled for April, 1923. Owing to his illness, Lenin could only dictate for a short time each day, and the main body of this letter was therefore composed in short bits on December 23-25, 1922, with the addition of a supplement—usually called the "Postscript"—dictated on January 4, 1923. The following is the entire "Testament" and "Postscript" (but not the other portions of the letter). In the interest of clarity the typographical arrangement of the dates of the parts of the letter has been altered from the original.

24 DECEMBER 1922

By the stability of the Central Committee, of which I spoke before, I mean measures to prevent a split, so far as such measures can be taken. For, of course, the White Guard in *Russkaia Mysl* [*Russian Thought*] (I think it was S. E. Oldenburg) was right when, in the first place, in his play against Soviet Russia he counted on the hope of a split in our party, and when, in the second place, he counted on that split as the result of serious disagreements in our party.

Our party rests upon two classes, and for that reason its instability is possible and its collapse is inevitable if agreement cannot be established between these two classes. In that event it would be useless to take any measures or in general to discuss the stability of our Central Committee. In that event no measures would prove capable of preventing a split. But I trust that is too remote a prospect, and too improbable an event, to talk about.

I have in mind stability as a guarantee against a split in the near future, and I intend to examine here a series of considerations of a purely personal character.

I think that the fundamental factor in the matter of stability—from this point of view—is such members of the Central Committee as Stalin and Trotsky. The relation between them constitutes, in my opinion, a big half of the danger of that split, which might be avoided, and the avoid-

From "Lenin's Testament." *The Department of State Bulletin*, XXXV, No. 891 (1956). 154-155, as revised by the editor of this book in the light of the Russian edition: Lenin, *Sochineniia*, XXXVI (Moscow: State Publishing House of Political Literature, 1957), 544-46.

ance of which, in my opinion, might be promoted, among other means, by raising the number of members of the Central Committee to fifty or one hundred.

Comrade Stalin, having become General Secretary, has concentrated enormous power in his hands; and I am not sure that he always knows how to use that power with sufficient caution. On the other hand Comrade Trotsky, as was proved by his struggle against the Central Committee in connection with the question of the People's Commissariat of Ways of Communication, is distinguished not only by his remarkable abilities. Personally he is very likely the ablest person in the present Central Committee, but he also is excessively self-confident and excessively attracted by the purely administrative side of affairs.

These two qualities of the two most able leaders of the present Central Committee might inadvertently lead to a split and if our party does not take measures to prevent it, a split might arise unexpectedly.

I will not further characterize the other members of the Central Committee as to their personal qualities. I will only remind you that the October episode of Zinoviev and Kamenev [they opposed a *coup* in 1917—*ed.*] was not, of course, accidental, but that it ought as little to be used against them personally as the non-Bolshevism of Trotsky.

Of the younger members of the Central Committee I want to say a few words about Bukharin and Piatakov. They are, in my opinion, the most able forces (among the youngest), and in regard to them it is necessary to bear in mind the following: Bukharin is not only the most valuable and most important theoretician of the party; but also may rightly be considered the favorite of the whole party; but his theoretical views can only with the very greatest reserve be regarded as fully Marxist, for there is something scholastic in them (he never has studied, and I think never has fully understood, dialectics). [End of dictation on this day—*ed.*]

DECEMBER 25

And then Piatakov—a man undoubtedly distinguished in will and remarkable ability, but too much given over to administration and the administrative side of things to be relied upon in a serious political question.

Of course, both these remarks are made by me merely with a view to the present time, on the assumption that these two able and loyal workers [Bukharin and Piatakov—*ed.*] may find occasion to increase their knowledge and correct their one-sidedness.

4 JANUARY 1923 [POSTSCRIPT—ed.]

Stalin is too rude, and this fault, entirely supportable in relations among us Communists, becomes insupportable in the office of General

Secretary. Therefore, I propose to the comrades to consider a way to remove Stalin from that position and appoint to it another man who in all respects differs from Stalin in one superiority—namely, that he be more tolerant, more loyal, more polite and more considerate to comrades, less capricious, etc. This circumstance may seem an insignificant trifle, but I think that from the point of view of preventing a split and from the point of view of the relation between Stalin and Trotsky which I discussed above, it is not a trifle, or it is such a trifle as may acquire decisive importance.

Lenin

STALIN

THE OCTOBER UPHEAVAL AND THE
QUESTION OF THE NATIONALITIES

During Lenin's lifetime Stalin was active in the service of the party, but in the main his writings were so close to those of Lenin that they do not cast much independent illumination on the major issues in Bolshevism. In one field, however, Stalin became established as the leading party spokesman in his own right while Lenin lived. This was the field of nationality affairs, the problems related to the multinational make-up of the Russian Empire and Soviet state. A Georgian by birth and a party organizer in the ethnically varied Caucasian area, Stalin possessed unusual qualifications in this field, and Lenin in 1913 encouraged his follower to contribute a substantial essay on the question of nationality to a leading Social Democratic periodical. Usually known as "Marxism and the National Question," this essay is probably Stalin's best-known work on the subject, but in retrospect it seems less important to the evolution of Bolshevik policy than some of Stalin's postrevolutionary writings. The point is that in 1913 it was still possible for Stalin to assert that the question of nationality was mainly a phenomenon of capitalism and would be a dead issue by the time the Social Democrats took power. Therefore Stalin's explanation of the Bolshevik position on nationality affairs—especially the right of nations to self-determination—was somewhat remote from the conditions that he had to face after his appointment as Peoples' Commissar of Nationality Affairs in November, 1917.

Soon after the Bolsheviks took power it became obvious that the question of nationality, far from disappearing with capitalism, was threatening to restrict the authority of the Bolshevik government to the comparatively limited area inhabited by the Great Russian people alone. Stalin faced a problem of unexpected dimensions and was obliged to play a major role in the formulation and execution of a policy that would reconstitute a multinational state while preserving some semblance of democracy. In working out this problem Stalin followed Lenin closely at times but in a number of instances disagreed with the leader, taking a more bluntly centralist approach than Lenin desired.

The following excerpt from an article of November 19, 1918, reflects this tendency in Stalin. While the "right of nations to self-determination" had been proclaimed by the Bolsheviks, Stalin announced that only the "toiling masses" could exercise this right; since only the Bolsheviks were supposed to represent the masses, this was tantamount to saying that there would be no national independence for borderlands in which the Bolshevik party opted for union with Moscow, as it invariably did. Lenin had criticized Stalin's formulation when it first appeared in January, 1918, but this did not deter his Commissar of Nationality Affairs from maintaining essentially the same position in the following statement and elsewhere.

At the same time the article reflects the assimilation into Bolshevik tactical doctrine of Lenin's belief that nationalist movements *outside* the Soviet sphere should be supported regardless of their social character as long as they embarrassed "imperialism."

In the period of the bourgeois revolution in Russia (February 1917) the national movement in the borderlands bore the character of a bourgeois liberation movement. The nationalities of Russia, which for ages had been oppressed and exploited by the "old regime," for the first time felt their strength and rushed into the fight with their oppressors. "Abolish national oppression"—such was the slogan of the movement. "All-national" institutions sprang up overnight throughout the borderlands of Russia. The movement was headed by the national, bourgeois-democratic intelligentsia. . . .

The right of nations to self-determination was interpreted as the right of the national bourgeoisie in the borderlands to take power into their own hands and to take advantage of the February Revolution for forming "their own" national states. The further development of the revolution did not and could not come within the calculations of the abovementioned bourgeois institutions. And the fact was overlooked that tsarism was being replaced by naked and barefaced imperialism, and that this imperialism was a stronger and more dangerous foe of the nationalities and the basis of a new national oppression.

The abolition of tsarism and the accession to power of the bourgeoisie did not, however, lead to the abolition of national oppression. The old, crude form of national oppression was replaced by a new, refined, but all the more dangerous, form of national oppression, the Lvov-Miliukov-Kerensky [Provisional] Government organized a new campaign against Finland (dispersal of the Diet in the summer of 1917) and the Ukraine (suppression of Ukrainian cultural institutions). What is more, that

From "The October Upheaval and the Question of the Nationalities." Stalin, *Works* (Moscow: Foreign Languages Publishing House, 1952-1955), IV, 158-70. The title given in this Soviet edition is not the one originally borne by the article, but the original appears here in translation.

government, which was imperialist by its very nature, called upon the population to continue the war in order to subjugate new lands, new colonies and nationalities. It was compelled to do this, not only because of the intrinsic nature of imperialism, but also because of the existence of the old imperialist states in the West, which were irresistibly striving to subjugate new lands and nationalities and threatening to narrow its sphere of influence. A struggle of the imperialist states for the subjugation of small nationalities as a condition for the existence of these states —such was the picture which was revealed in the course of the imperialist war. . . .

Thus, the old bourgeois-democratic interpretation of the principle of national self-determination became a fiction and lost its revolutionary significance. It was clear that under such circumstances there could be no question of the abolition of national oppression and [of] establishing the independence of the small national states. It became obvious that the emancipation of the laboring masses of the oppressed nationalities and the abolition of national oppression were inconceivable without a break with imperialism, without the laboring masses overthrowing "their own" national bourgeoisie and taking power themselves. . . .

Having triumphed in the center of Russia and embraced a number of the borderlands, the October Revolution could not stop short at the territorial borders of Russia. In the atmosphere of the imperialist world war and the general discontent among the masses, it could not but spread to neighboring countries. Russia's break with imperialism and its escape from the predatory war; the publication of the secret treaties and the solemn renunciation of the policy of annexations; the proclamation of the national freedom and recognition of the independence of Finland; the declaring of a "federation of Soviet national republics" by Russia and the battle cry of a determined struggle against imperialism issued to the world by the Soviet government—all this could not but deeply affect the enslaved East and the bleeding West.

And indeed, the October Revolution is the first revolution in world history to break the age-long sleep of the laboring masses of the oppressed peoples of the East and to draw them into the fight against world imperialism. The formation of workers' and peasants' Soviets in Persia, China and India, modelled on the Soviets in Russia, is sufficiently convincing evidence of this. . . .

The chief point is not at all that the struggle in the East and even in the West has not yet succeeded in shedding its bourgeois-nationalist features; the point is that the struggle against imperialism *has begun,* that it is continuing and is inevitably bound to arrive at its logical goal.

Foreign intervention and the occupation policy of the "external" imperialists merely sharpen the revolutionary crisis, by drawing new peoples into the struggle and extending the area of the revolutionary battles with imperialism.

Thus, the October Revolution, by establishing a tie between the peoples of the backward East and the advanced West, is ranging them in a common camp of struggle against imperialism.

Thus, from the particular question of combating national oppression, the question of nationality is evolving into the general question of emancipating the nations, colonies and semi-colonies from imperialism.

ON THE DEATH OF LENIN

When Lenin died on January 21, 1924, following almost two years of intermittent illness, Stalin could not yet attempt to succeed to the supreme leadership in the Bolshevik Party and Soviet state. It is true that he held a variety of powerful offices, especially that of Secretary General of the Central Committee of the party. But he could not yet dictate to the other leading members of the party, such as Trotsky, Zinoviev, Kamenev, and Bukharin, and in any case it would have been tactless and risky for any individual to attempt to assert himself as a replacement for the venerated founder of Bolshevism.

In such circumstances Stalin's best course was to make no specific move to extend his power but to present himself as the most reverent mourner and faithful executor of the departed leader. This was a sound self-introduction to the rank and file of party members who had so far not thought of Stalin as an eminent leader, and it was an especially useful image to impress upon the more than 200,000 new members who were taken into the party at Stalin's instance as "The First Lenin Enrolment," conducted in the months immediately following Lenin's funeral. These new Bolsheviks, predominantly workers of rather simple intellectual background, contributed powerfully to the ascent of Stalin in the next few years, and it was to such as they that he directed the simple, liturgical intonations of the eulogy. For a man who is usually, and often rightly, considered a poor orator, it was a highly effective performance, especially in the absence of competition from the leading orator of the revolution and the most renowned Bolshevik next to Lenin—Leon Trotsky. This leader was at the time in the Caucasus for a rest cure and, according to his testimony, was deliberately misinformed by Stalin concerning the date of the funeral in order to dissuade him from appearing among the mourners (and heirs).

The following speech was delivered by Stalin not at the bier itself, although he was conspicuous there as a silent pallbearer and guard of honor, but at a special meeting of Congress of Soviets on January 26 in honor of Lenin. His body was placed on display in a temporary public mausoleum. Subsequently a permanent, public mausoleum containing the preserved body of the leader was opened on Red Square, a symbol of bolshevism and the achievements of scientific socialism—or at least socialist mortuary science.

Comrades, we Communists are people of a special mold. We are made of a special stuff. We are those who form the army of the great proletarian strategist, the army of Comrade Lenin. There is nothing higher than the honor of belonging to this army. There is nothing higher than the title of member of the party whose founder and leader was Comrade Lenin. It is not given to everyone to be a member of such a party. It is not given to everyone to withstand the stresses and storms that accompany membership in such a party. It is the sons of the working class, the sons of want and struggle, the sons of incredible privation and heroic effort who before all should be members of such a party. That is why the party of the Leninists, the party of the Communists, is also called the party of the working class.

Departing from us, Comrade Lenin enjoined us to hold high and guard the purity of the great title of member of the party. We vow to you, Comrade Lenin, that we shall fulfill your behest with honor!

For twenty-five years Comrade Lenin tended our party and made it into the strongest and most highly steeled workers' party in the world. The blows of tsarism and its henchmen, the fury of the bourgeoisie and the landlords, the armed attacks of Kolchak and Denikin [commanders of anti-Bolshevik armies—*ed.*], the armed intervention of Britain and France, the lies and slanders of the hundred-mouthed bourgeois press— all these scorpions constantly chastised our party for a quarter of a century. But our party stood firm as a rock, repelling the countless blows of its enemies and leading the working class forward, to victory. In fierce battles our party forged the unity and solidarity of its ranks. And by unity and solidarity it achieved victory over the enemies of the working class. *Departing from us, Comrade Lenin enjoined us to guard the unity of our party and the apple of our eye. We vow to you, Comrade Lenin, that this behest, too, we shall fulfill with honor!* . . .

Like a huge rock, our country stands out amid an ocean of bourgeois states. Wave after wave dashes against it, threatening to submerge it and wash it away. But the rock stands unshakable. Wherein lies its strength? Not only in the fact that our country rests on an alliance of the workers and peasants, that it embodies a union of free nationalities, that it is protected by the mighty arm of the Red Army and the Red Navy. The strength, the firmness, the solidity of our country is due to the profound sympathy and unfailing support it finds in the hearts of the workers and peasants of the whole world. The workers and peasants of the whole world want to preserve the Republic of Soviets as an arrow shot by the sure hand of Comrade Lenin into the camp of the enemy, as the pillar of their hopes of deliverance from oppression and exploitation, as a reliable beacon pointing the path to their emancipation. They want to preserve it, and they will not allow the landlords and capitalists to destroy it. Therein lies our strength. Therein lies the strength of the working people of all countries. And therein lies the weakness of the bourgeoisie all over the world.

Lenin never regarded the Republic of Soviets as an end in itself. He always looked on it as an essential link for strengthening the revolutionary movement in the countries of the West and the East, an essential link for facilitating the victory of the working people of the whole world over capitalism. Lenin knew that this was the only right conception, both from the international standpoint and from the standpoint of preserving the Republic of Soviets itself. Lenin knew that this alone could fire the hearts of the working people of the whole world with determination to fight the decisive battles for their emancipation. That is why, on the very morrow of the establishment of the dictatorship of the proletariat, he, the greatest of the geniuses who have led the proletariat, laid the foundation of the workers' International. That is why he never tired of extending and strengthening the union of the working people of the whole world—the Communist International.

You have seen during the past few days the pilgrimage of scores and hundreds of thousands of working people to Comrade Lenin's bier. Before long you will see the pilgrimage of representatives of millions of working people to Comrade Lenin's tomb. You need not doubt that the representatives of millions will be followed by representatives of scores and hundreds of millions from all parts of the earth, who will come to testify that Lenin was the leader not only of the Russian proletariat, not only of the European workers, not only of the colonial East, but of all the working people of the globe.

Departing from us, Comrade Lenin enjoined us to remain faithful to the principles of the Communist International. We vow to you, Comrade Lenin, that we shall not spare our lives to strengthen and extend the union of the working people of the whole world—the Communist International!

THE FOUNDATIONS OF LENINISM

Stalin lost little time in enlarging his stature as the first Leninist in the party. In April and May, 1924, he presented a series of lectures on "The Foundations of Leninism," which reverently summarized Lenin's leading ideas without any pretense of innovation. The principal audience was intended to be the younger and inexperienced party members, for the lectures were delivered at Sverdlov University, dedicated to the "Lenin Enrolment." They were accompanied by the publication, in the magazine *Red Youth*, of a "Plan of a Seminar of Leninism," which contained a detailed reading syllabus, and they were widely disseminated in pamphlets and in anthologies throughout the rest of Stalin's career, serving as a primer for successive classes of young Bolsheviks.

The nine lectures range over most of the major aspects of Bolshevik ideology, but the following selection, an interpretation of Lenin's theory of imperialism, is of special importance as a guide to Stalin's appreciation of the future chances for Communist revolution. Clearly he placed great emphasis on the necessity of such revolutions: necessity in the sense that the laws of history make revolutions inevitable, and necessity in the narrower sense that the Soviet Union depends on the spread of revolution for its own security. In fact, Stalin initially stressed Russian dependence on foreign revolution more than he meant to. The original version of the last paragraph quoted below states that a solitary revolutionary country like Russia cannot even organize socialist production. By the close of 1924 Stalin was maintaining a different view of the possibility of "socialism in one country" (see the next selection). He then found his remarks in "The Foundations of Leninism" inconvenient and soon altered them to read as they are printed here. The incident is noteworthy because it shows clearly that this teacher of Leninism was concerned with the manipulation as well as the dissemination of Lenin's ideas.

The Leninist theory of the proletarian revolution proceeds from three fundamental theses.

From "The Foundations of Leninism." Stalin, *Works*, VI, 71-196.

First Thesis: The domination of finance capital in the advanced capitalist countries; the issue of stocks and bonds as one of the principal operations of finance capital; the export of capital to the sources of raw materials, which is one of the foundations of imperialism; the omnipotence of a financial oligarchy, which is the result of the domination of finance capital—all this reveals the grossly parasitic character of monopolist capitalism, makes the yoke of the capitalist trusts and syndicates a hundred times more burdensome, it intensifies the indignation of the working class with the foundations of capitalism, and brings the masses to the proletarian revolution as their only salvation. . . .

Hence the first conclusion: intensification of the revolutionary crisis within the capitalist countries and growth of the elements of an explosion of the internal proletarian front in the "mother countries."

Second Thesis: The increase in the export of capital to the colonies and dependent countries; the expansion of "spheres of influence" and colonial possessions until they cover the whole globe; the transformation of capitalism into a world system of financial enslavement and colonial oppression of the overwhelming majority of the population of the world by a handful of "advanced" countries—all this has, on the one hand, converted the separate national economics and national territories into links in a single chain called world economy, and, on the other hand, split the population of the globe into two camps: a handful of "advanced" capitalist countries which exploit and oppress vast colonies and dependencies, and the vast majority consisting of colonial and dependent countries which are compelled to fight for their liberation from the imperialist yoke (see *Imperialism*).

Hence the second conclusion: intensification of the revolutionary crisis in the colonial countries and growth of the elements of revolt against imperialism on the external, colonial front.

Third Thesis: The monopolistic possession of "spheres of influence" and colonies; the uneven development of capitalist countries, leading to a frenzied struggle for the redivision of the world between the countries which have already seized territories and those claiming their "share"; imperialist wars as the only means of restoring the disturbed "equilibrium"—all this leads to the intensification of the struggle on the third front, the inter-capitalist front, which weakens imperialism and facilitates the amalgamation of the first two fronts against imperialism: the front of the revolutionary proletariat and the front of colonial emancipation.

Hence the third conclusion: that under imperialism wars cannot be averted, and that a coalition between the proletarian revolution in Europe and the colonial revolution in the East in a united world front of revolution against the world front of imperialism is inevitable.

Leninism combines all these conclusions into one general conclusion that *"imperialism is the eve of the socialist revolution."*

The very approach to the question of the proletarian revolution, of the character of the revolution, of its scope, of its depth, the scheme of the revolution in general, changes accordingly.

Formerly, the analysis of the prerequisites for the proletarian revolution was usually approached from the point of view of the economic state of individual countries. Now this approach is no longer adequate. Now the matter must be approached from the point of view of the economic state of all or the majority of countries, from the point of view of the state of world economy; for individual countries and individual national economies have ceased to be self-sufficient units, have become links in a single chain called world economy; for the old "cultured" capitalism has evolved into imperialism, and imperialism is a world system of financial enslavement and colonial oppression of the vast majority of the population of the earth by a handful of "advanced" countries.

Formerly it was the accepted thing to speak of the existence or absence of objective conditions for the proletarian revolution in individual countries, or, to be more precise, in one or another developed country. Now this point of view is no longer adequate. Now we must speak of the existence of objective conditions for the revolution in the entire system of world imperialist economy as an integral unit; the existence within this system of some countries that are not sufficiently developed industrially cannot serve as an insurmountable obstacle to the revolution, if the system as a whole, or, more correctly, because the system as a whole is already ripe for revolution.

Formerly it was the accepted thing to speak of the proletarian revolution in one or another developed country as of a separate and self-sufficient entity opposing a separate national front of capital as its antipode. Now, this point of view is no longer adequate. Now we must speak of the world proletarian revolution; for the separate national fronts of capital have become links of a single chain called the world front of imperialism, which must be opposed by a common front of the revolutionary movement in all countries.

Formerly the proletarian revolution was regarded exclusively as the result of the internal development of a given country. Now, this point of view is no longer adequate. Now the proletarian revolution must be regarded primarily as the result of the development of the contradictions within the world system of imperialism, as the result of the breaking of the chain of the imperialist world front in one country or another.

Where will the revolution begin? Where, in what country, can the front of capital be pierced first?

Where industry is more developed, where the proletariat constitutes the majority where there is more culture, where there is more democracy —that was the reply usually given formerly.

No, objects the Leninist theory of revolution; *not necessarily where industry is more developed*, and so forth. The front of capital will be pierced where the chain of imperialism is weakest, for the proletarian revolution is the result of the breaking of the chain of the world imperialist front at its weakest link; and it may turn out that the country which has started the revolution, which has made a breach in the front of capital, is less developed in a capitalist sense than other more developed countries, which have, however, remained within the framework of capitalism.

In 1917 the chain of the imperialist world front proved to be weaker in Russia than in the other countries. It was there that the chain gave way and provided an outlet for the proletarian revolution. Why? Because in Russia a great popular revolution was unfolding, and at its head marched the revolutionary proletariat, which has such an important ally as the vast mass of the peasantry who were oppressed and exploited by the landlords. Because the revolution there was opposed by such a hideous representative of imperialism as tsarism, which lacked all moral prestige and was deservedly hated by the whole population. The chain proved to be weaker in Russia, although that country was less developed in a capitalist sense than say, France or Germany, England or America.

Where will the chain break in the near future? Again, where it is weakest. It is not precluded that the chain may break, say, in India. Why? Because that country has a young, militant, revolutionary proletariat, which as such an ally as the national liberation movement—an undoubtedly powerful and undoubtedly important ally. Because there the revolution is confronted by such a well-known foe as foreign imperialism, which lacks all moral credit and is deservedly hated by the oppressed and exploited masses of India.

It is quite possible that the chain will break in Germany. Why? Because the factors which are operating, say, in India are beginning to operate in Germany as well; but of course, the enormous difference in the level of development between India and Germany cannot but stamp its imprint on the progress and outcome of a revolution in Germany. . . .

But the overthrow of the power of the bourgeoisie and establishment of the power of the proletariat in one country does not yet mean that the complete victory of socialism has been ensured. After consolidating its power and leading the peasantry in its wake the proletariat of the victorious country can and must build a socialist society. But does this mean that it will thereby achieve the complete and final victory of socialism, i.e., does it mean that with the forces of only one country it can finally consolidate socialism and fully guarantee that country against intervention and, consequently, also against restoration? No, it does not.

For this the victory of the revolution in at least several countries is needed. Therefore, the development and support of revolution in other countries is an essential task of the victorious revolution. Therefore, the revolution which has been victorious in one country must regard itself not as self-sufficient entity, but as an aid, as a means for hastening the victory of the proletariat in other countries.

Lenin expressed this thought succinctly when he said that the task of the victorious revolution is to do "the utmost possible in one country *for* the development, support, and awakening of the revolution *in all countries.*"

These, in general, are the characteristic features of Lenin's theory of proletarian revolution.

THE OCTOBER REVOLUTION AND THE TACTICS OF THE RUSSIAN COMMUNISTS

The seventh anniversary of the Bolshevik Revolution in the fall of 1924 produced a round of commemorative publications by leading Bolsheviks, which served as polemical weapons in the competition for succession to supreme leadership. At this time Trotsky, the outstanding individual leader, faced a coalition of Kamenev, Zinoviev, and Stalin, who collectively held the upper hand. Trotsky opened the conflict with a collection of his writings of 1917, prefaced by an attack on the wavering behavior of Kamenev and Zinoviev just before the October Revolution. His opponents replied in kind, Stalin's contribution being an anthology entitled "On the Road to October," which he prefaced with an essay of unusual doctrinal and polemical importance.

Entitled "The October Revolution and the Tactics of the Russian Communists," this work attempted to combine emphasis on the importance of revolution abroad with emphasis on the possibility of building "socialism in one country" (i.e., Soviet Russia). Although Stalin's debating form was as heavy-handed as usual, the line of attack was shrewdly chosen. Trotsky, like Lenin, hoped for the early success of proletarian revolution abroad, but, with the failure of an attempted revolution in Germany in the fall of 1923, this hope receded into the indefinite future. Some adjustment in Bolshevik doctrine was needed if general pessimism was to be avoided, and Stalin, for all his supposed clumsiness as a theoretician, reacted to the situation with more agility than any other Bolshevik leader.

He dropped the view that the development of a socialist economy in Russia would require foreign revolutionary aid, and even revised his sermon on "The Foundations of Leninism" to this effect (see p. 76). He maintained instead that both the strength of the worker-peasant alliance in Russia and the internal weakness of imperialism made it possible to accomplish a great deal in building socialism even if revolution was long in coming to Europe. To show, as Stalin wished to, that Lenin explicitly supported this doctrine required some rather strained exegesis, but the argument no doubt appealed to the self-esteem and Russian nationalism of many Bolsheviks. Under the circumstances it was a more optimistic doctrine than Trotsky's "permanent revolution," the belief that the Russian revolution would ignite a series of European revolutions, which would make possible the construction of socialism in Russia. With a bit of twisting, Stalin was even able to maintain that Trotsky lacked faith in world revolution as well as in Russian socialism, an artful distortion that few debaters could have achieved. So well did the slogan "socialism in one country" serve Stalin that it became one of his major articles of faith following the publication of this essay in January, 1925.

There are two specific features of the October Revolution which must be understood first of all if we are to comprehend the inner meaning and the historical significance of that revolution.

What are these features?

Firstly, the fact that the dictatorship of the proletariat was born in our country as a power which came into existence on the basis of an alliance between the proletariat and the laboring masses of the peasantry, the latter being led by the proletariat. Secondly, the fact that the dictatorship of the proletariat became established in our country as a result of the victory of socialism in one country—a country in which capitalism was little developed—while capitalism was preserved in other countries where capitalism was more highly developed. This does not mean, of course, that the October Revolution has no other specific features. But it is precisely these two specific features that are important for us at the present moment, not only because they distinctly express the essence of the October Revolution, but also because they brilliantly reveal the opportunist nature of the theory of "permanent revolution."

Let us briefly examine these features.

The question of the laboring masses of the petty bourgeoisie, both urban and rural, the question of winning these masses to the side of the proletariat, is highly important for the proletarian revolution. Whom will the laboring people of town and country support in the struggle for power, the bourgeoisie or the proletariat; whose reserve will they become, the reserve of the bourgeoisie or the reserve of the proletariat— on this depends the fate of the revolution and the stability of the dictatorship of the proletariat. The revolutions in France in 1848 and 1871 came to grief chiefly because the peasant reserves proved to be on the side of the bourgeoisie. The October Revolution was victorious because it was able to deprive the bourgeoisie of its peasant reserves, because it was able to win these reserves to the side of the proletariat, and because

From "The October Revolution and the Tactics of the Russian Communists." Stalin, *Works*, VI, 374-420.

in this revolution the proletariat proved to be the only guiding force for the vast masses of the laboring people of town and country. . . .

The dictatorship of the proletariat is not simply a governmental top stratum "skillfully selected" by the careful hand of an "experienced strategist," and "judiciously relying" on the support of one section or another of the population. The dictatorship of the proletariat is the class alliance between the proletariat and the laboring masses of the peasantry for the purpose of overthrowing capital, for achieving the final victory of socialism, on the condition that the guiding force of this alliance is the proletariat.

Lenin speaks of the *alliance* between the proletariat and the laboring strata of the peasantry as the basis of the dictatorship of the proletariat. Trotsky sees a *"hostile collision"* between "the proletarian vanguard" and "the broad masses of the peasantry."

Lenin speaks of the *leadership* of the toiling and exploited masses by the proletariat. Trotsky sees *"contradictions* in the position of a workers' government in a backward country with an overwhelmingly peasant population."

According to Lenin, the revolution draws its strength primarily from among the workers and peasants of Russia itself. According to Trotsky, the necessary strength can be found *only* "in the arena of the world proletarian revolution."

But what if the world revolution is fated to arrive with some delay? Is there any ray of hope for our revolution? Trotsky offers no ray of hope, for "the contradictions in the position of a workers' government . . . could be solved *only* . . . in the arena of the world proletarian revolution." According to this plan, there is but one prospect left for our revolution: to vegetate in its own contradictions and rot away while waiting for the world revolution. . . .

What difference is there between this "theory of permanent revolution" and the well-known theory of Menshevism which repudiates the concept of dictatorship of the proletariat?

Essentially, there is no difference.

There can be no doubt at all. "Permanent revolution" is not a mere underestimation of the revolutionary potentialities of the peasant movement. "Permanent revolution" is an underestimation of the peasant movement which leads to the *repudiation* of Lenin's theory of the dictatorship of the proletariat.

Trotsky's "permanent revolution" is a variety of Menshevism. . . .

What is the second specific feature of the October Revolution?

The second specific feature of the October Revolution lies in the fact that this revolution represents a model of the practical application of Lenin's theory of the proletarian revolution. . . .

The opportunists of all countries assert that the proletarian revolution can begin—if it is to begin anywhere at all, according to their theory—only in industrially developed countries, and that the more highly developed these countries are industrially the more chances there are for the victory of socialism. Moreover, according to them, the possibility of the victory of socialism in one country, and one in which capitalism is little developed at that, is excluded as something absolutely improbable. As far back as the period of the war, Lenin, taking as his basis the law of the uneven development of the imperialist states, opposed to the opportunists his theory of the proletarian revolution about the victory of socialism in one country, even if that country is one in which capitalism is less developed.

It is well-known that the October Revolution fully confirmed the correctness of Lenin's theory of the proletarian revolution.

How do matters stand with Trotsky's "permanent revolution" in the light of Lenin's theory of the victory of the proletarian revolution in one country?

Let us take Trotsky's pamphlet *Our Revolution* (1906).

Trotsky writes:

"Without direct state support from the European proletariat, the working class of Russia will not be able to maintain itself in power and to transform its temporary rule into a lasting socialist dictatorship. This we cannot doubt for an instant."

What does this quotation mean? It means that the victory of socialism in one country, in this case Russia, is impossible "*without* direct state support from the European proletariat," i.e., before the European proletariat has conquered power.

What is there in common between this "theory" and Lenin's thesis on the possibility of the victory of socialism "in one capitalist country taken separately"?

Clearly, there is nothing in common. . . .

It goes without saying that for the *complete* victory of socialism, for a *complete* guarantee against the restoration of the old order, the united efforts of the proletarians of several countries are necessary. It goes without saying that, without the support given to our revolution by the proletariat of Europe, the proletariat of Russia could not have held out against the general onslaught, just as without the support given by the revolution in Russia to the revolutionary movement in the West the latter could not have developed at the pace at which it has begun to develop since the establishment of the proletarian dictatorship in Russia.

It goes without saying that we need support. But what does support of our revolution by the West-European proletariat imply? Is not the sympathy of the European workers for our revolution, their readiness to thwart the imperialists' plans of intervention—is not all this support, real assistance? Unquestionably it is. Without such support, without such assistance, not only from the European workers but also from the colonial and dependent countries, the proletarian dictatorship in Russia would have been hard pressed. Up to now, has this sympathy and this assistance, coupled with the might of our Red Army and the readiness of the workers and peasants of Russia to defend their socialist fatherland to the last—has all this been sufficient to beat off the attacks of the imperialists and to win us the necessary conditions for the serious work of construction? Yes it has been sufficient. Is this sympathy growing stronger, or is it waning? Unquestionably, it is growing stronger. Hence, have we favorable conditions, not only for pushing on with the organising of socialist economy, but also, in our turn, for giving support to the West-European workers and to the oppressed peoples of the East? Yes, we have. This is eloquently proved by the seven years' history of the proletarian dictatorship in Russia. Can it be denied that a mighty wave of labor enthusiasm has already risen in our country? No, it cannot be denied.

After all this, what does Trotsky's assertion that a revolutionary Russia could not hold out in the face of a conservative Europe signify?

It can signify only this: firstly, that Trotsky does not appreciate the inherent strength of our revolution; secondly, that Trotsky does not understand the inestimable importance of the moral support which is given to our revolution by the workers of the West and the peasants of the East; thirdly, that Trotsky does not perceive the internal infirmity which is consuming imperialism today. . . .

Lack of faith in the strength and capacities of our revolution, lack of faith in the strength and capacity of the Russian proletariat—that is what lies at the root of the theory of "permanent revolution."

Hitherto only *one* aspect of the theory of "permanent revolution" has usually been noted—lack of faith in the revolutionary potentialities of the peasant movement. Now, in fairness, this must be supplemented by *another* aspect—lack of faith in the strength and capacity of the proletariat in Russia.

What difference is there between Trotsky's theory and the ordinary Menshevik theory that the victory of socialism in one country, and in a backward country at that, is impossible without the preliminary victory of the proletarian revolution "in the principal countries of Western Europe?"

Essentially, there is no difference.

There can be no doubt at all. Trotsky's theory of "permanent revolution" is a variety of Menshevism.

CONCERNING QUESTIONS
OF LENINISM

By the opening of 1926, Trotsky had been outmaneuvered in the opening round of the competition for succession to supreme party leadership, and Stalin, aligned now with Bukharin and others, was engaged in a struggle with Zinoviev. The rivalry was conducted in the realm of ideology and in the regional party organizations, especially in Leningrad, which was the main stronghold of Zinoviev supporters. In a whirlwind campaign of January, 1926, Stalin's group won over the majority of the rank-and-file party members in that city, paving the way for the removal of the leading Zinovievites. Evidently Stalin was preparing a substantial polemical essay, a portion of which follows, to hurl into the fray. But by January 25, the date of its completion, Leningrad was already in Stalin's hands, and he was able to heap humiliation on his defeated rival by dedicating the essay to the Leningrad party organization.

In the course of raking Zinoviev for his interpretation of the dictatorship of the proletariat, Stalin explained his conception of the party's dominant role in this system, something Lenin had failed to do in his "State and Revolution." The gist of this fundamental Stalinist conception follows.

Now we must deal with the dictatorship of the proletariat from the point of view of its structure, from the point of view of its "mechanism," from the point of view of the role and significance of the "transmission belts," the "levers," and the "directing force" which in their totality constitute "the system of the dictatorship of the proletariat" (Lenin), and with the help of which the daily work of the dictatorship of the proletariat is accomplished.

What are these "transmission belts" or "levers" in the system of the dictatorship of the proletariat? What is this "directing force"? Why are they needed?

The levers or the transmission belts are those very mass organizations of the proletariat without whose aid the dictatorship cannot be realized.

The directing force is the advanced detachment of the proletariat, its

From "Concerning Questions of Leninism." Stalin, *Works*, VIII, 13-96.

vanguard which is the main guiding force of the dictatorship of the proletariat.

The proletariat needs these transmission belts, these levers, and this directing force, because without them, in its struggle for victory, it would be a weaponless army in the face of organized and armed capital. The proletariat needs these organizations because without them it would suffer inevitable defeat in its fight for the overthrow of the bourgeoisie, in its fight for the consolidation of its own power, in its fight for the building of socialism. The systematic help of these organizations and the directing force of the vanguard are indispensable because without them a dictatorship of the proletariat to any extent durable and firm is impossible.

What are these organizations?

First, there are the workers' trade unions, with their central and local ramifications in the shape of a whole series of industrial, cultural, educational, and other organizations. These unite the workers of all trades. They are non-party organizations. The trade unions may be termed the all-embracing organizations of the working class which is in power in our country. They are a school of communism. They promote the best people from their midst to carry on leading work in all branches of administration. They form the link between the advanced and the backward elements in the ranks of the working class. They connect the masses of the workers with the vanguard of the working class.

Secondly, there are the Soviets and their numerous central and local ramifications in the shape of administrative, economic, military, cultural, and other state organizations, plus the innumerable voluntary mass associations of the working people which group themselves around these organizations of all the working people of town and country. They are non-party organizations. The Soviets are the direct expression of the dictatorship of the proletariat. It is through the Soviets that all and sundry measures for strengthening the dictatorship and for building socialism are carried out. It is through the Soviets that the state leadership of the peasantry by the proletariat is exercised. The Soviets connect the millions of working people with the vanguard of the proletariat.

Thirdly, there are the cooperative societies of all kinds, with all their ramifications. These are mass organizations of working people, non-party organizations, which unite the working people primarily as consumers, but also, in the course of time, as producers (agriculture cooperation). The cooperative societies assume special significance after the consolidation of the dictatorship of the proletariat during the period of extensive construction. They facilitate contact between the vanguard of the proletariat and the masses of the peasantry and provide the possibility of drawing the latter into the channel of socialist construction.

Fourthly, there is the Youth League [Komsomol]. This is a mass organization of young workers and peasants; it is a non-party organization, but it is associated with the party. Its task is to help the party to educate the young generation in the spirit of socialism. It provides young reserves for all the other mass organizations of the proletariat in all branches of administration. The Youth League has acquired special significance since the consolidation of the dictatorship of the proletariat, in the period of extensive cultural and educational work carried on by the proletariat.

Lastly, there is the party of the proletariat, its vanguard. Its strength lies in the fact that it draws into its ranks all the best elements of the proletariat from all the mass organizations of the proletariat. Its function is to combine the work of all the mass organizations of the proletariat without exception and to direct their activities towards a single goal, the goal of the emancipation of the proletariat. And it is absolutely necessary that they be combined and directed towards a single goal, for otherwise unity in the struggle of the proletariat is impossible, for otherwise the guidance of the proletarian masses in their struggle for power, in the struggle for the building of socialism, is impossible. But only the vanguard of the proletariat, its party, is capable of combining and directing the work of the mass organizations of the proletariat, only the Communist Party is capable of fulfilling this role of main leader in the system of the dictatorship of the proletariat. . . .

THE TROTSKYIST OPPOSITION
BEFORE AND NOW

Probably the most determined attempt by Stalin's opponents to stop his march to supremacy occurred about the time of the tenth anniversary of the Bolshevik Revolution in 1927. The former rivals Trotsky and Zinoviev, both having lost earlier rounds to Stalin, now pooled their forces and attempted to use every available weapon to shake Stalin's hold on the leading organs of the party. Their efforts included publication of an anti-Stalin platform, agitation in local party bodies, attempted public demonstrations in Moscow and Leningrad, and the revival of Lenin's testamentary statements against Stalin.

The Secretary General met them firmly at every point and succeeded in neutralizing the opposition, preparatory to finishing it off in the somewhat deferred Party Congress of December, 1927. His particular stronghold was the carefully prepared joint meeting of the Central Executive Committee and Central Control Commission, convened in October. Here he gave one of his characteristic oratorical performances, turning his opponents' attack into rout, ending with the expulsion of Trotsky and Zinoviev from the Central Committee. As indicated by the interjections from the floor during Stalin's speech of October 23, his audience was predisposed to accept his crushing indictment of those who threatened to split the monolithic party.

It is said that in that "will" Comrade Lenin suggested that in view of Stalin's "rudeness" it [the Twelfth Party Congress] should consider the question of putting another comrade in Stalin's place as General Secretary. That is quite true. [Let us read that passage, although it has already been read repeatedly at the plenary session—(*Stalin reads the first two sentences of the postscript of Lenin's will, dated Dec. 25, 1922;* see p. 91).]

From "The Trotskyist Opposition Before and Now." Stalin, *Works*, X, 177-211. When the *Works* were published after the Second World War, Stalin no longer faced an audience that included persons who had Lenin's "Testament" in their possession and so Stalin chose not to quote directly from it. Therefore the bracketed material near the beginning of this oration was omitted from the *Works*. It did however appear in the first published version of the speech, in *Pravda*, November 2, 1927.

Yes, comrades, I am rude to those who grossly and perfidiously wreck and split the party. I have never concealed this and do not conceal it now. Perhaps some mildness is needed in the treatment of splitters, but I am a bad hand, at that. At the very first meeting of the plenum of the Central Committee after the Thirteenth Congress I asked the plenum of the Central Committee to release me from my duties as General Secretary. The congress itself discussed this question. It was discussed by each delegation separately, and all the delegations unanimously, including Trotsky, Kamenev, and Zinoviev, obliged Stalin to remain at his post.

What could I do? Desert my post? That is not in my nature; I have never deserted any post, and I have no right to do so, for that would be desertion. As I have already said before, I am not a free agent, and when the party imposes an obligation upon me, I must obey.

A year later I again put in a request to the plenum to release me, but I was again obliged to remain at my post.

What else could I do?

As regards publishing the "will," the Congress decided not to publish it, since it was addressed to the Congress and was not intended for publication.

We have the decision of a plenum of the Central Committee and Central Control Commission in 1926 to ask the Fifteenth Congress [for] permission to publish this document. We have the decision of the same plenum of the Central Committee and Central Control Commission to publish other letters of Lenin's, in which he pointed out the mistakes of Kamenev and Zinoviev just before the October uprising and demanded their expulsion from the party.

Obviously, talk about the party concealing these documents is infamous slander. Among these documents are letters from Lenin urging the necessity of expelling Zinoviev and Kamenev from the party. The Bolshevik Party, the Central Committee of the Bolshevik Party, have never feared the truth. The strength of the Bolshevik Party lies precisely in the fact that it does not fear the truth and looks the truth straight in the face.

The opposition is trying to use Lenin's "will" as a trump card; but it is enough to read this "will" to see that it is not a trump card for them at all. On the contrary, Lenin's "will" is fatal to the present leaders of the opposition.

Indeed, it is a fact that in his "will" Lenin accuses Trotsky of being guilty of "non-Bolshevism" and, as regards the mistake Kamenev and Zinoviev made during October, he says that that mistake was not "accidental." What does that mean? It means that Trotsky, who suffers from "non-Bolshevism," and Kamenev and Zinoviev, whose mistakes are not "accidental" and can and certainly will be repeated, cannot be politically trusted.

It is characteristic that there is not a word, not a hint in the "will" about Stalin having made mistakes. It refers only to Stalin's rudeness. But rudeness is not and cannot be counted as a defect in Stalin's political line or position.

Here is the relevant passage in the "will":

"I will not further characterize the other members of the Central Committee as to their personal qualities. I will only remind you that the October episode of Zinoviev and Kamenev was not, of course, accidental, but that it ought as little to be used against them personally as the non-Bolshevism of Trotsky."

Clear, one would think. . . .

Zinoviev and Trotsky vehemently asserted here that we are preparing for the Congress by means of a repression. It is strange that they see nothing but "repression." But what about the decision to open a discussion taken by a plenum of the Central Committee and Central Control Commission more than a month before the congress—is that in your opinion preparation for the Congress, or is it not? And what about the discussion in the party units and other party organizations that has been going on incessantly for three of four months already? And the discussion of the verbatim reports and decisions of the plenum that has been going on for the past six months, particularly the past three or four months, on all questions concerning home and foreign policy? What else can all this be called if not stimulating the activity of the party membership, drawing it into the discussion of the major questions of our policy, preparing the party membership for the Congress?

Who is to blame if, in all this, the party organizations do not support the opposition? Obviously, the opposition is to blame, for its line is one of utter bankruptcy, its policy is that of a bloc with all the anti-party elements, including the renegades Maslow and Souvarine [ex-Communists in Germany and France—*ed.*], against the party and the Comintern.

Evidently, Zinoviev and Trotsky think that preparations for the Congress ought to be made by organizing illegal, anti-party printing presses, by organizing illegal, anti-party meetings, by supplying false reports about our party to the imperialists of all countries, by disorganizing and splitting our party. You will agree that this is a rather strange idea of what preparations for the Party Congress mean. And when the party takes resolute measures, including expulsion, against the disorganizers and splitters, the opposition raises a howl about repression.

Yes, the party resorts and will resort to repression against disorganizers and splitters, for the party must not be split under any circumstances, either before the Congress or during the Congress. It would be suicidal for the party to allow out-and-out splitters, the allies of all sorts of Shcherbakovs [Bolshevik expelled for illegal opposition—*ed.*], to wreck the party just because only a month remains before the Congress.

Comrade Lenin saw things in a different light. You know that in 1921 Lenin proposed that [G.] Shliapnikov [member of "Workers' Opposition," 1921—*ed.*] be expelled from the Central Committee and from the party not for organizing an anti-party printing press, and not for allying himself with bourgeois intellectuals, but merely because, at a meeting of a party unit, Shliapnikov dared to criticize the decisions of the Supreme Council of National Economy. If you compare this attitude of Lenin's with what the party is now doing to the opposition, you will realize what license we have allowed the disorganizers and splitters.

You surely must know that in 1917, just before the October uprising, Lenin several times proposed that Kamenev and Zinoviev be expelled from the Party merely because they had criticized unpublished Party decisions in the semi-socialist, in the semi-bourgeois newspaper *Novaia Zhizn* (*The New Life*). But how many secret decisions of the Central Committee and the Central Control Commission are now being published by our opposition in the columns of Maslow's newspaper in Berlin, which is a bourgeois anti-Soviet, counter-revolutionary newspaper! Yet we tolerate all this, tolerate it without end, and thereby give the splitters in the opposition the opportunity to wreck our party. Such is the disgrace to which the opposition has brought us! But we cannot tolerate it forever, comrades. (Voices: "Quite right!" Applause.)

It is said that disorganizers who have been expelled from the party and conduct anti-Soviet activities are being arrested. Yes, we arrest them, and we shall do so in future if they do not stop undermining the party and the Soviet regime. (Voices: "Quite right! Quite right!")

It is said that such things are unprecedented in the history of our party. That is not true. What about the Miasnikov group? What about the "Workers' Truth" group? Who does not know that the members of those groups were arrested with the full consent of Zinoviev, Trotsky, and Kamenev? Why was it permissible three or four years ago to arrest disorganizers who had been expelled from the party, but is impermissible now, when some of the former members of the Trotskyist opposition go to the length of directly linking up with counter-revolutionaries?

You heard Comrade Menzhinsky's [head of secret police—*ed.*] statement. In that statement it is said that a certain Stepanov (an army-man), a member of the party, a supporter of the opposition, is in direct contact with counter-revolutionaries, with Novikov, Kostrov, and others, which Stepanov himself does not deny in his depositions.* What do you want us to do with this fellow, who is in the opposition to this day? Kiss him, or arrest him? Is it surprising that the OGPU [secret police—*ed.*] arrests such fellows? (Voices from the audience: "Quite right! Absolutely right!" Applause.)

Lenin said that the party can be completely wrecked if indulgence is shown to disorganizers and splitters. That is quite true. That is precisely why I think that it is high time to stop showing indulgence to the leaders of the opposition and to come to the conclusion that Trotsky and Zi-

---

* He was a provateur planted by the police—*ed.*

noviev must be expelled from the Central Committee of our party. (Voices: "Quite right!") That is the elementary conclusion and the elementary, minimum measure that must be taken in order to protect the party from the disorganizers' splitting activities.

At the last plenum of the Central Committee and Central Control Commission, held in August this year, some members of the plenum rebuked me for being too mild with Trotsky and Zinoviev, for advising the plenum against the immediate expulsion of Trotsky and Zinoviev from the Central Committee. (Voices from the audience: "That's right, and we rebuke you now.") Perhaps I was too kind then and made a mistake in proposing that a milder line be adopted towards Trotsky and Zinoviev. (Voices: "Quite right!" Comrade Petrovsky: "Quite right. We shall always rebuke you for being soft to factionalists!") But now, comrades, after what we have gone through during these three months, after the opposition has broken the promise to dissolve its faction that it made in its special "declaration" of August 8, thereby deceiving the party once again, after all this, there can be no more room at all for mildness. We must now step into the front rank with those comrades who are demanding that Trotsky and Zinoviev be expelled from the Central Committee. (Stormy applause. Voices: "Quite right! Quite right!" A voice from the audience: "Trotsky should be expelled from the party.") Let the Congress decide that, comrades.

In expelling Trotsky and Zinoviev from the Central Committee we must submit for the consideration of the Fifteenth Congress all the documents which have been accumulated concerning the opposition's splitting activities, and on the basis of those documents the Congress will be able to adopt an appropriate decision.

CONCERNING QUESTIONS
OF AGRARIAN POLICY
IN THE USSR

Behind the Bolshevik Revolution, behind the new Soviet state, behind Stalin and his rivals, loomed the perennial peasant-agrarian question. How should the millions of Russian peasants be treated to maximize food production and Communist political objectives? In October, 1917, Lenin had come to power with a Decree on Land that temporarily gave the peasants the free use of virtually all arable land, which is to say that it extended temporary approval to what the peasants were already doing in practice. This, however, was a political expedient to suit a situation in which the party could not dictate to the peasants and needed their acquiescence. Since the Decree on Land generally led to the rise of private peasant farms, it was not compatible with the long-term collectivist goal of communism. But in Lenin's lifetime and in the ensuing five years, the necessity of staving off famine at any price and the need to build up the instruments of party rule prevented as well as inhibited any major program of transformation on the countryside.

True, Trotsky, Zinoviev, and others argued that the peasants, especially the more prosperous ones (*kulaks*), should be pressured by taxation and price regulation into yielding a larger marketable surplus to support increasing industrialization, but Stalin and especially his ally Bukharin had argued that the most practical policy for the time being was to encourage the peasants to produce more under the relatively free enterprise of the New Economic Policy.

However, when the Trotsky-Zinoviev group had been quashed and when peasant-grain marketings fell dangerously low in 1927-1928, Stalin turned away from his moderate agrarian line and its supporter Bukharin. In the course of 1929 Stalin outmaneuvered Bukharin and his supporters, removing them from most of their high offices, and increasingly pressed for a harder line against the kulaks and for the rapid development of collectivized agriculture.

On December, 1929, Stalin's unchallenged supremacy in the party was acknowledged in connection with the celebration of his fiftieth birthday, and, almost simultaneously, he intensified his campaign of collectivization and dekulakization to a revolutionary pitch that nobody (even Stalin, perhaps) had anticipated. Of his various statements on the agrarian question at about this time his speech of December 27, 1929, "Concerning Questions of Agrarian Policy in the USSR," is probably the most crucial because of its call for the "elimination of the kulaks as a class." In the following two months the party leaders in the field interpreted "kulak" so loosely and collectivized other peasants with such abandon that Stalin himself had to call for a respite by March. But even if the campaign had exceeded his intent and even if the impact on agrarian production (especially livestock herds) was serious for years to come as a result of this disruption, Stalin seems to have been satisfied with the fundamental results: the liquidation of the more prosperous peasants and the subjection of peasants to a collective form that greatly enhanced the control of the party machinery over the peasant and the fruits of his labor.

Comrades, the main fact of our social and economic life at the present time, a fact which is attracting universal attention, is the tremendous growth of the collective-farm movement.

The characteristic feature of the present collective-farm movement is that not only are the collective farms being joined by individual groups of poor peasants, as has been the case hitherto, but that they are being joined by the mass of the middle peasants as well. This means that the collective-farm movement has been transformed from a movement of individual groups and sections of the laboring peasants into a movement of millions and millions of the main mass of the peasantry. This, by the way, explains the tremendously important fact that the collective-farm movement, which has assumed the character of a mighty and growing *anti-kulak* avalanche, is sweeping the resistance of the kulak from its path, is shattering the kulak class, and [is] paving the way for extensive socialist construction in the countryside. . . .

Until recently, the peasant was compelled to dig the soil with old-fashioned implements by individual labor. Everyone knows that individual labor, equipped with old-fashioned, now unsuitable, instruments of production, does not bring the gains required to enable one to lead a tolerable existence, systematically improve one's material position, develop one's culture, and emerge on to the high road of socialist construction. Today, after the accelerated development of the collective-farm movement, the peasants are able to combine their labor with that of their neighbors, to unite in collective farms, to plough virgin soil, to utilize neglected land, to obtain machines and tractors and thereby

From "Concerning Questions of Agrarian Policy in the USSR." Stalin, *Works*, XII, 147-78.

double or even treble the productivity of labor. And what does this mean? It means that today the peasant, by joining the collective farm, is able to produce much more than formerly with the same expenditure of labour. It means, therefore, that grain will be produced much more cheaply than was the case until quite recently. It means, finally, that with stable prices, the peasant can obtain much more for his grain than he has obtained up to now.

How, after all this, can it be asserted that the October Revolution brought no gains to the peasantry?

Is it not clear that those who utter such fictions obviously slander the Party and the Soviet power?

But what follows from all this?

It follows that the question of the "scissors," the question of doing away with the "scissors,"* must now be approached in a new way. It follows that if the collective-farm movement grows at the present rate, the "scissors" will be abolished [price equilibrium will be restored—*ed.*] in the near future. It follows that the question of the relations between town and country is now put on a new basis, that the antithesis between town and country will disappear at an accelerated pace.

This circumstance, comrades, is of very great importance for our whole work of construction. It transforms the mentality of the peasant and turns him towards the town. It creates the basis for eliminating the antithesis between town and country. It creates the basis for the slogan of the party—"face to the countryside"—to be supplemented by the slogan of the peasant collective farmers: "face to the town."

Nor is there anything surprising in this, for the peasant is now receiving from the town machines, tractors, agronomists, organizers and, finally, direct assistance in fighting and [in] overcoming the kulaks. The old type of peasant, with his savage distrust of the town, which he regarded as plunderer, is passing into the background. His place is being taken by the new peasant, by the collective-farm peasant, who looks to the town with the hope of receiving real assistance in *production*. The place of the old type of peasant who was afraid of sinking to the level of the poor peasants and only stealthily (for he could be deprived of the franchise!) rose to the position of a kulak, is being taken by the new peasant, with a new prospect before him—that of joining a collective farm and emerging from poverty and ignorance on to the high road of economic and cultural progress.

Finally, the question of the class changes in our country and the offensive of socialism against the capitalist elements in the countryside.

The characteristic feature in the work of our Party during the past year is that we, as a party, as the Soviet power:

---

* The decline in the price of agricultural goods and increase in the price of industrial goods, so-called because of the appearance of these changes on a chart.

(a) have developed an offensive along the whole front against the capitalist elements in the countryside;

(b) that this offensive, as you know, has yielded and continues to yield very appreciable, *positive* results.

What does this mean? It means that we have passed from the policy of *restricting* the exploiting tendencies of the kulaks to the policy of *eliminating* the kulaks as a class. It means that we have carried out, and are continuing to carry out, one of the decisive turns in our whole policy.

Until recently the party adhered to the policy of *restricting* the exploiting tendencies of the kulaks. As you know, this policy was proclaimed as far back as the Eighth Party Congress. It was again announced at the time of the introduction of the NEP and at the Eleventh Congress of our party. We all remember Lenin's well-known letter about Preobrazhensky's [a Bolshevik economist—*ed.*] theses (1922), in which Lenin once again returned to the need for pursuing this policy. Finally, this policy was confirmed by the Fifteenth Congress of our party. And it was this policy that we were pursuing until recently.

Was this policy correct? Yes, it was absolutely correct at the time. Could we have undertaken such an offensive against the kulaks some five years or three years ago? Could we then have counted on success in such an offensive? No, we could not. That would have been the most dangerous adventurism. It would have been a very dangerous playing at an offensive. For we should certainly have failed, and our failure would have strengthened the position of the kulaks. Why? Because we did not yet have in the countryside strong points in the form of a wide network of state farms and collective farms which could be the basis for a determined offensive against the kulaks. Because at that time we were not yet able to *replace* the capitalist production of the kulaks by the socialist production of the collective farms and state farms. . . .

What would it have meant to launch a determined offensive against the kulaks under such conditions? It would have meant certain failure, strengthening the position of the kulaks and being left without grain. That is why we could not and should not have undertaken a determined offensive against the kulaks at that time, in spite of the adventurist declamations of the Zinoviev-Trotsky opposition.

But today? What is the position now? Today, we have an adequate material base for us to strike at the kulaks, to break their resistance, to eliminate them as a class, and to *replace* their output by the output of the collective farms and state farms. You know that in 1929 the grains produced on the collective farms and state farms has amounted to not less than 400,000,000 puds (200,000,000 puds less than the gross output of the kulak farms in 1927) [one pud equals 36 pounds—*ed.*]. You also know that in 1929 the collective farms and state farms have supplied more than 130,000,000 puds of marketable grain (i.e., more than the kulaks in 1927). Lastly, you know that in 1930 the gross output of the collective farms and state farms will amount to not less than 900,000,000 puds of grain (i.e., more than the gross output of the kulaks in 1927), and their output of marketable grain will be not less than 400,000,000 puds (i.e., incomparably more than the kulaks supplied in 1927).

That is how matters stand with us now, comrades.

There you have the change that has taken place in the economy of our country.

Now, as you see, we have the material base which enables us to *replace* the kulak output by the output of the collective farms and state farms. It is for this very reason that our determined offensive against the kulaks is now meeting with undeniable success.

That is how an offensive against the kulaks must be carried on, if we mean a genuine and determined offensive and not mere futile declamations against the kulaks.

That is why we have recently passed from the policy of *restricting* the exploiting tendencies of the kulaks to the policy of *eliminating* the kulaks as a class.

Well, and what about the policy of dekulakization? Can we permit dekulakization in the areas of complete collectivization? This question is asked in various quarters. A ridiculous question! We could not permit dekulakization as long as we were pursuing the policy of restricting the exploiting tendencies of the kulaks, as long as we were unable to go over to a determined offensive against the kulaks, as long as we were unable to replace the kulak output by the output of the collective farms and state farms. At that time the policy of not permitting dekulakization was necessary and correct. But now? Now things are different. Now we are able to carry on a determined offensive against the kulaks, break their resistance, eliminate them as a class, and replace their output by the output of the collective farms and state farms. Now, dekulakization is being carried out by the masses of poor and middle peasants themselves, who are putting complete collectivization into practice. Now, dekulakization in the areas of complete collectivization is no longer just an administrative measure. Now, it is an integral part of the formation and development of the collective farms. Consequently it is now *ridiculous* and foolish to discourse at length on dekulakization. When the head is off, one does not mourn for the hair.

There is another question which seems no less ridiculous: whether the kulaks should be permitted to join the collective farms. Of course not, for they are sworn enemies of the collective-farm movement. . . .

ON THE TASKS OF INDUSTRIAL ADMINISTRATORS

Along with the campaign of intensive collectivization of agriculture, the first years following Stalin's emergence as supreme leader were marked by a colossal effort to increase industrial production. Of course, the growth of state-owned, state-directed industrial economy had been accepted as an axiom by all Bolsheviks and envisaged in rather rosy terms by Lenin's electrification project. In April, 1929, the party officially approved a "Five-Year Plan" as the vehicle of this development, but this comparatively modest program was soon swamped by a series of much more ambitious goals, accompanied by the Stalinist slogan "the Five-Year Plan in four years."

To press home this drive—which did, although it was really incapable of complete fulfillment, produce major achievements in some branches of industry—the party had to be thrown into industrial administration and the technical experts had to be Bolshevized more than ever before. Stalin addressed himself to this task in a major speech at a conference of "workers [mainly administrators and engineers] of socialist industry" on February 4, 1931, which was roughly the time of maximum exertion in the First Five-Year Plan.

It is significant that Stalin's appeal for Bolshevik, revolutionary ardor in industrial development is combined with a strong tug at Great Russian nationalist sentiments. The approach is clearly not one of Russian nationalism *instead of* communism, but rather Russian nationalism and communism *in fusion*. Although there is precedent for this outlook in earlier statements by Lenin and Stalin, it was only after about 1930 and the opening of the Stalinized Five-Year Plans that official recognition of the glory of Russian nationalism was clearly and loudly proclaimed. The sense of continuity between the traditional interests of the Russian nation and communism was elsewhere reflected in revised party attitudes toward the writing of history, the Russian literary heritage, and even the Orthodox Church. This tendency grew fairly steadily throughout the Thirties, was greatly strengthened during the "Great Fatherland War of the Soviet Union" (World War II), and reached its apogee in the years 1946-1948 under the immediate auspices of Stalin's lieutenant A. A. Zhdanov.

Comrades, the deliberations of your conference are drawing to a close. You are now about to adopt resolutions. I have no doubt that they will be adopted unanimously. In these resolutions—I am somewhat familiar with them—you approve the control figures of industry for 1931 and pledge yourselves to fulfil them.

A Bolshevik's word is his bond. Bolsheviks are in the habit of filfilling promises made by them. But what does the pledge to fulfil the control figures for 1931 mean? It means ensuring a total increase of industrial output by 45 per cent. And that is a very big task. More than that. Such a pledge means that you not only pledge yourselves to fulfil our five-year plan in four years—that matter has already been settled, and no more resolutions on it are needed—*it means that you promise to fulfil it in three years in all the basic, decisive branches of industry. . . .*

It is sometimes asked whether it is not possible to slow down the tempo somewhat, to put a check on the movement. No, comrades, it is not possible! The tempo must not be reduced! On the contrary, we must increase it as much as is within our powers and possibilities. This is dictated to us by our obligations to the workers and peasants of the USSR. This is dictated to us by our obligations to the working class of the whole world.

To slacken the tempo would mean falling behind. And those who fall behind get beaten. But we do not want to be beaten. No, we refuse to be beaten! One feature of the history of old Russia was the continual beatings she suffered because of her backwardness. She was beaten by the Mongol khans. She was beaten by the Turkish beys. She was beaten by the Swedish feudal lords. She was beaten by the Polish and Lithuanian gentry. She was beaten by the British and French capitalists. She was beaten by the Japanese barons. All beat her—because of her backwardness, because of her military backwardness, cultural backwardness, political backwardness, industrial backwardness, agricultural backwardness. They beat her because to do so was profitable and could be done with impunity. You remember the words of the pre-revolutionary poet: "You are poor and abundant, mighty and impotent, Mother Russia." * Those gentlemen were quite familiar with the verses of the old poet. They beat her, saying: "You are abundant," so one can enrich oneself at your expense. They beat her, saying: "You are poor and impotent," so you can be beaten and plundered with impunity. Such is the law of the exploiters—to beat the backward and the weak. It is the jungle law of capitalism. You are backward, you are weak—therefore you are wrong;

From "On the Tasks of Industrial Administrators." Stalin, *Works*, XIII, 31-44.
* From the poem "Who Lives Happily in Russia?" (1876) by N. A. Nekrasov—*ed.*

hence you can be beaten and enslaved. You are mighty—therefore you are right; hence we must be wary of you.

That is why we must no longer lag behind.

In the past we had no fatherland, nor could we have had one. But now that we have overthrown capitalism and power is in our hands, in the hands of the people, we have a fatherland, and we will uphold its independence. Do you want our socialist fatherland to be beaten and to lose its independence? If you do not want this, you must put an end to its backwardness in the shortest possible time and develop a genuine Bolshevik tempo in building up its socialist economy. There is no other way. That is why Lenin said on the eve of the October Revolution: "Either perish, or overtake and outstrip the advanced capitalist countries."

We are fifty or a hundred years behind the advanced countries. We must make good this distance in ten years. Either we do it, or we shall go under.

That is what our obligations to the workers and peasants of the USSR dictate to us.

But we have yet other, more serious and more important, obligations. They are our obligations to the world proletariat. They coincide with our obligations to the workers and peasants of the USSR. But we place them higher. The working class of the USSR is part of the world working class. We achieved victory not solely through the efforts of the working class of the USSR, but also thanks to the support of the working class of the world. Without this support we would have been torn to pieces long ago. It is said that our country is the shock brigade of the proletariat of all countries. That is well said. But it imposes very serious obligations upon us. Why does the international proletariat support us? How did we merit this support? By the fact that we were the first to hurl ourselves into the battle against capitalism, we were the first to establish working-class state power, we were the first to begin building socialism. By the fact that we are engaged on a cause which, if successful, will transform the whole world and free the entire working class. But what is needed for success? The elimination of our backwardness, the development of a high Bolshevik tempo of construction. We must march forward in such a way that the working class of the whole world, looking at us, may say: There you have my advanced detachment, my shock brigade, my working-class state power, my fatherland; they are engaged on their cause, *our* cause, and they are working well; let us support them against the capitalists and promote the cause of the world revolution. Must we not justify the hopes of the world's working class, must we not fulfil our obligations to them? Yes, we must if we do not want to utterly disgrace ourselves.

Such are our obligations, internal and international. As you see, they dictate to us a Bolshevik tempo of development.

I will not say that we have accomplished nothing in regard to management of production during these years. In fact, we have accomplished a good deal. We have doubled our industrial output compared with the pre-war level. We have created the largest-scale agricultural production in the world. But we could have accomplished still more if we had tried during this period really to master production, the technique of production, the financial and economic side of it.

In ten years at most we must make good the distance that separates us from the advanced capitalist countries. We have all the "objective" possibilities for this. The only thing lacking is the ability to make proper use of these possibilities. And that depends on us. *Only* on us! It is time we learned to make use of these possibilities. It is time to put an end to the rotten line of non-interference in production. It is time to adopt a new line, one corresponding to the present period—the line of *interfering in everything*. If you are a factory director—interfere in all the affairs of the factory, look into everything, let nothing escape you, learn and learn again. Bolsheviks must master technique. It is time Bolsheviks themselves became experts. In the period of reconstruction, technique decides everything. And an industrial administrator who does not want to study technique, who does not want to master technique, is a joke and not an administrator.

It is said that it is hard to master technique. That is not true! There are no fortresses that Bolsheviks cannot capture. We have solved a number of most difficult problems. We have overthrown capitalism. We have assumed power. We have built up a huge socialist industry. We have transferred the middle peasants on to the path of socialism. We have already accomplished what is most important from the points of view of construction. What remains to be done is not so much: to study technique, to master science. And when we have done that we shall develop a tempo of which we dare not even dream at present.

And we shall do it if we really want to.

ON THE DRAFT CONSTITUTION
OF THE USSR

The terrific sacrifices endured by the Soviet populace during the early years of collectivization and rapid industrialization were not recompensed by a generally visible rise in the standard of living (on the contrary, there was a sharp decline in some respects), but Stalin was too shrewd to overlook the need for some definite monument to the achievements of his regime. This took the form of a jubilant assertion that the Soviet Union (impoverished and constrained as its people might be) had passed a major milestone: socialism on the path to the most perfect of human societies, fully-developed communism. This claim was embodied in a new constitution, a component of the "superstructure" in Marxist terms, inevitably reflecting the major changes in the economic "base" in Soviet Russia.

The adoption of the new constitution was heralded by a staggering publicity campaign, starting well before the official enactment of the new constitution on December 5, 1936, and lasting in considerable strength for years afterwards. The warm-up included wide dissemination of the first public draft of the new constitution for party-directed "discussion" around the country, leading up to a special session of the All-Union Congress of Soviets in November, 1936, at which Stalin on the 25th of that month commented on the criticism and suggestions that had come forth in the previous months. With some changes that he approved, the document was adopted and frantically hailed as the "Stalin Constitution." This was ironic designation considering that much of the document was drafted by Bukharin, the defeated rival of Stalin, who had been partially rehabilitated in 1936 and was to die as a "traitor" in 1938.

The new government structure (not party organization, which was unchanged) was formally more democratic than the system in force during the years 1924-1936. For example, the former system of unequal and indirect suffrage, supposedly needed to fend off bourgeois interests, was replaced by a system of equal and direct suffrage. But, as Stalin said, this change reflected not a desire for open political competition but rather the party's conviction that the party no longer need fear dissent among the people.

. . . What are the principal specific features of the Draft Constitution submitted for consideration to the present Congress?

The Constitution Commission was instructed to amend the text of the Constitution of 1924. The work of the Constitution Commission has resulted in a new text of the Constitution, a Draft of a new Constitution of the USSR. In drafting the new Constitution, the Constitution Commission proceeded from the premise that a constitution must not be confused with a program. This means that there is an essential difference between a program and a constitution. Whereas a program speaks of that which does not yet exist, of that which has already been achieved and won now, at the present time. A program deals mainly with the future, a constitution with the present.

Two examples by way of illustration.

Our Soviet society has already, in the main, succeeded in achieving socialism; it has created a socialist system, i.e., it has brought about what Marxists in other words call the first, or lower phase, of communism. Hence, in the main, we have already achieved the first phase of communism, socialism. (Prolonged applause.) The fundamental principle of this phase of communism is, as you know, the formula: "From each according to his ability, to each according to his work." Should our Constitution reflect this fact, the fact that socialism has been achieved? Should it be based on this achievement? Unquestionably, it should. It should, because for the USSR socialism is something already achieved and won.

But Soviet society has not yet reached the higher phase of communism, in which the ruling principle will be the formula: "From each according to his ability, to each according to his needs," although it sets itself the aim of achieving the higher phase of communism in the future. Can our Constitution be based on the higher phase of communism, which does not yet exist and which has still to be achieved? No, it cannot, because that has not yet been realized, and which has to be realized in the future. It cannot, if it is not to be converted into a program or a declaration of future achievements.

Such are the limits of our Constitution at the present historical moment.

Thus, the Draft of the new Constitution is a summary of the path that has been traversed, a summary of the gains already achieved. In other words, it is the registration and legislative embodiment of what has already been achieved and won in actual fact. (Loud applause.) . . .

I must admit that the Draft of the new Constitution does preserve the regime of the dictatorship of the working class, just as it also preserves unchanged the present leading position of the Communist Party

From "On the Draft Constitution of the USSR." Stalin, *Problems of Leninism* (Moscow: Foreign Languages Publishing House, 1953), pp. 679-712.

of the USSR. (Loud applause.) If the esteemed critics regard this as a flaw in the Draft Constitution, that is only to be regretted. We Bolsheviks regard it as a merit of the Draft Constitution. (Loud applause.)

As to freedom for various political parties, we adhere to somewhat different views. A party is a part of a class, its most advanced part. Several parties, and, consequently, freedom for parties, can exist only in a society in which there are antagonistic classes whose interests are mutually hostile and irreconcilable—in which there are, say, capitalists and workers, landlords, and peasants, kulaks and poor peasants, etc. But in the USSR there are no longer such classes as the capitalists, the landlords, the kulaks, etc. In the USSR there are only two classes, workers and peasants, whose interests—far from being mutually hostile—are, on the contrary, friendly. Hence, there is no ground in the USSR for the existence of several parties, and, consequently, for freedom for these parties. In the USSR there is ground only for one party, the Communist Party. In the USSR only one party can exist, the Communist Party, which courageously defends the interests of the workers and peasants to the very end. And that it defends the interests of these classes not at all badly, of that there can hardly be any doubt. (Loud applause.)

They talk of democracy. But what is democracy? Democracy in capitalist countries, where there are antagonistic classes, is, in the last analysis, democracy for the strong, democracy for the propertied minority. In the USSR, on the contrary, democracy is democracy for the working people, i.e., democracy for all. But from this it follows that the principles of democratism are violated, not by the Draft of the new Constitution of the USSR, but by the bourgeois constitutions. That is why I think that the Constitution of the USSR is the only thoroughly democratic Constitution in the world.

Such is the position with regard to the bourgeois criticism of the Draft of the new Constitution of the USSR. . . .

Judging by the results of the nation-wide discussion, which lasted nearly five months, it may be presumed that the Draft Constitution will be approved by the present Congress. (Loud applause passing into an ovation. All rise.)

In a few days' time the Soviet Union will have a new, socialist Constitution, built on the principles of fully developed socialist democratism.

It will be an historic document dealing in simple and concise terms, almost in the style of minutes, with the facts of the victory of socialism in the USSR, with the facts of the emancipation of the working people of the USSR from a capitalist slavery, with the facts of the victory in the USSR of full and thoroughly consistent democracy.

It will be a document testifying to the fact that what millions of honest people in capitalist countries have dreamed of and still dream of has already been realized in the USSR. (Loud applause.)

It will be a document testifying to the fact that what has been realized in the USSR is fully possible of realization in other countries also. (Loud applause.)

But from this it follows that the international significance of the new Constitution of the USSR can hardly be exaggerated.

Today, when the turbid wave of fascism is bespattering the socialist movement of the working class and besmirching the democratic aspirations of the best people in the civilized world, the new Constitution of the USSR will be an indictment against fascism, declaring that socialism and democracy are invincible. (Applause.) The new Constitution of the USSR will give moral assistance and real support to all those who are today fighting fascist barbarism. (Loud applause.)

Still greater is the significance of the new Constitution of the USSR for the peoples of the USSR. While for the peoples of capitalist countries the Constitution of the USSR will have the significance of a program of action, it is significant for the peoples of the USSR as the summary of their struggles, a summary of their victories in the struggle for the emancipation of mankind. After the path of struggle and privation that has been traversed, it gives pleasure and happiness to have our Constitution, which treats of the fruits of our victories. It gives pleasure and happiness to know what our people fought for and how they achieved this victory of world-wide historical importance. It gives pleasure and happiness to know that the blood our people shed so plentifully was not shed in vain, that it has produced results. (Prolonged applause.) This arms our working class, our peasantry, our working intelligentsia spiritually. It impels them forward and rouses a sense of legitimate pride. It increases confidence in our strength and mobilizes us for fresh struggles for the achievement of new victories of communism. (Thunderous ovation. All rise. A thunderous "Hurrah!" Shouts from all parts of the hall: "Long live Comrade Stalin!" All stand and sing the "International," after which the ovation is resumed. Shouts of "Long live our leader, Comrade Stalin, Hurrah!")

ON DEFICIENCIES IN PARTY WORK AND MEASURES FOR LIQUIDATING TROTSKYISTS AND OTHER DOUBLE-DEALERS

While the "Stalin Constitution" was being hailed as a sign of the end of class conflict in Soviet Union, the Stalin regime was fanatically concerned with what it alleged to be the extirpation of a plot by class-enemies, foreign and Russian, to wreck the entire government and social system. The apparent contradiction between the glories of harmonious progress and the specter of widespread treason was reconciled by Stalin as an inevitable part of the path to utopia: as the imperialists lose ground they become more frantic in their attempts to counterattack. To what extent Stalin believed this theory and the accompanying charges of conspiracy against a wide range of old political opponents, distinguished military leaders, his own protégés, and others is impossible to know. But it is clear that, from the assassination of the party boss of Leningrad, Kirov, in December, 1934, until the end of 1938, Stalin was bent upon conducting a reign of terror that would drastically alter the membership of the higher echelons of the party and cow virtually all citizens who held positions of even moderate responsibility.

In the main he held himself aloof from personal, public participation in this campaign, although his propagandists constantly stressed that the death of the great Stalin was the crowning goal of the lurid machinations directed by the exiled Trotsky. But, at a crucial point in the development of the campaign of terror, Stalin found it necessary to justify his program to the party at large. When the Central Committee convened in February, 1937, there had already been two major "show trials" of former oppositionists, but Stalin insisted on spreading wider still the circle of accusations and executions. Since there seemed to be very little rational justification, even by the most ruthless standards of security, for further bloodletting, some of Stalin's own associates objected. The most distinguished of these dissenters was Sergo Ordzhonikidze, the leading industrial boss in the party, who was either murdered or harried into suicide before the opening of the Central Committee sessions. Others spoke against Stalin in the course of the secret meetings, and the leader evidently felt obliged to make it amply clear that he regarded an extension of the terror as an essential policy. If he offered no very convincing proof of the objective necessity of the terror, he left no doubt that every Bolshevik was bound to support it—or be regarded as one of the enemy.

Although the main speech by which Stalin attempted to assert absolutely his arbitrary will was delivered to the Central Committee on March 3-5, 1937, some tactical consideration persuaded or obliged him to postpone publication of it until March 29.

Comrades!
From the reports and the discussions of them at the plenary session [of the Central Committee], it is obvious that we have here a matter involving three basic facts.

First, the wrecking and diversionist-espionage work of the agents of foreign states, among whom the Trotskyists have played a rather active role, has touched to this or to that extent all or almost all of our organizations, both economic and administrative or party.

Second, the agents of foreign states, including Trotskyists, have penetrated not only into our lower organizations but also into some of the responsible positions.

Third, some of our leading comrades, both at the center and in outlying regions, have not only been unable to see the real face of these wreckers, diversionists, spies, and murderers but have proven to be careless, indifferent, and naïve about it, and not infrequently they have cooperated in promoting the agents of foreign states into this or that responsible position.

Such are the three indisputable facts which naturally follow from the reports and discussion on them.

How is one to explain that our leading comrades, who have rich experience in the struggle with all kinds of antiparty and antisoviet tendencies, have proven in this case so naïve and blind, and are unable to see the real face of the enemies of the people, unable to recognize the wolf in sheep's clothing, unable to unmask them?

Can we say that the wrecking and diversionist-espionage work of the agents of foreign states on the territory of the USSR is something unexpected and unprecedented for us? No, we cannot say this. . . .

Can we say that of late we have had no warning signals or advance indications concerning the wrecking, espionage, or terrorist activities

From "On Deficiencies in Party Work and Measures for Liquidating Trotskyists and Other Double-Dealers." *Pravda*, March 29, 1937. Editor's translation.

of the Trotskyist-Zinovievist agents of fascism? No, we cannot say this. . . .

How can one explain that our party comrades, despite their rich experience in the struggle with antisoviet elements, despite a whole series of warning signals and advance indications, have proven politically near-sighted in the face of the wrecking and espionage-diversionist work of the enemies of the people? . . .

The point is this, that our party comrades, having been wholly absorbed in the economic campaigns and the colossal successes on the economic construction front, simply forgot some very important facts that Bolsheviks have no right to forget. . . .

They forgot that Soviet power has conquered only in one-sixth of the earth, that five-sixths of the earth remains in the possession of capitalist states. They forgot that the Soviet Union finds itself in the circumstances of capitalist encirclement. . . .

Capitalist encirclement—this is not an empty phrase but a very real and disagreeable reality. Capitalist encirclement—this means that there is one country, the Soviet Union that by itself established a socialist order and [this means] that outside of this there are many countries, bourgeois countries, which continue to lead the capitalist order of life and which surround the Soviet Union, awaiting an opportunity to fall on it, to smash it, or in any case to undermine its power and to weaken it. . . .

Further, while struggling with Trotskyist agents, our party comrades did not notice, they overlooked that present-day Trotskyism is not what it was, say, seven or eight years ago, that Trotskyism and Trotskyists in this period underwent a major evolution, which has radically changed the face of Trotskyism, and that in view of this the struggle with Trotskyism and the methods of the struggle with it must be changed radically. Our party comrades have not noticed that Trotskyism has ceased to be a political tendency in the working class, that from a political tendency in the working class, which it was seven or eight years ago, Trotskyism has changed into a frantic and unprincipled band of wreckers, diversionists, spies, and murderers, acting under the orders of the intelligence organs of foreign states. . . .

In the trial in 1936, if you recall, Kamenev and Zinoviev definitely denied that they had any political platform. They had every chance to disclose to the court their political platform. However they did not do this, declaring that they had no platform. There can be no doubt that they both lied in denying that they had a platform. Now even the blind can see that they had a political platform. But why did they deny that they had a political platform? Because they feared to uncover their vile political character, they feared to show their real platform of restoring capitalism in the USSR, fearing that such a platform would arouse the disgust of the working class.

In the trial in 1937, Piatakov, Radek, and Sokolnikov took another course. They did not deny that the Trotskyists and Zinovievists had a political platform. They admitted that they had a political platform, admitted it and disclosed it in their testimony. They disclosed it not to summon the working class, to summon the people, to support the Trotskyist platform but to condemn and stigmatize it as an antipopular and antiproletarian platform. The restoration of capitalism, the liquidation of kolkhozes and sovkhozes [collective farms and state farms—*ed*.], the establishment of a system of exploitation, the alliance with the fascist forces of Germany and Japan to bring closer a war with the Soviet Union, the struggle for war and against the policy of peace, the territorial dismemberment of the Soviet Union with the award of the Ukraine to the Germans and the Maritime region [including Vladivostok—*ed*.] to the Japanese, the preparation of the military defeat of the Soviet Union in case of attack by hostile states, and, as a means of achieving these ends, the wrecking, diversion, individual terrorism against the leaders of the Soviet state, espionage on behalf of the Japanese-German forces— such was the platform of present-day Trotskyism disclosed by Piatakov, Radek, and Sokolnikov. . . .

What do we need to do?

It is necessary to realize the following measures.

1. First of all it is necessary to turn the attention of our party comrades who are absorbed with "current questions" from the line of this or that department to the side of the major political questions of an international or domestic character.

2. It is necessary to raise the political work of our party to the required level, giving the leading position to the task of the political enlightenment and Bolshevik hardening of party, Soviet, and economic cadres.

3. It is necessary to make it clear to our party comrades that economic successes, the significance of which is indisputably very great and which we will henceforth achieve day by day and year by year—that all this does not exhaust the whole matter of our socialist construction. . . .

4. It is necessary to remember and never to forget that capitalist encirclement is a basic fact which defines the international situation of the Soviet Union.

To remember and never forget that while there is capitalist encirclement there will be wreckers, diversionists, spies, terrorists who have been dispatched into the rear areas of the Soviet Union by the intelligence organs of foreign states. . . .

5. It is necessary to make clear to our party comrades that the Trotskyists, who represent an active element in the diversionist-wrecker and espionage work of foreign intelligence organs, have long since ceased to be a political tendency in the working class, that they have long

since ceased to serve any ideal corresponding to the interests of the working class, that they have changed into an unprincipled and un-idealistic band of wreckers, diversionists, spies, murderers, who are working as hirelings of foreign intelligence organs. . . .

6. It is necessary to make clear to our party comrades the difference between the contemporary wreckers and the wreckers of the Shakhty period [1928—the first trial of "wreckers"—engineers of the Shakhty coal mines—*ed.*], to make it clear that while the wreckers of the Shakhty period deceived our people in technical matters, making use of their technical backwardness, the contemporary wreckers, who have party membership cards, deceive our people by obtaining their confidence as members of the party, making use of the political carelessness of our people. . . .

7. It is necessary to smash and throw out the rotten theory that, with each forward movement that we make, the class struggle will die down more and more, that in proportion to our successes the class enemy will become more and more tame. This is not only a rotten theory but also a dangerous theory, for it lulls our people, leads them into a trap, and gives the class enemy a chance to prepare for struggle with the Soviet government.

On the contrary, the more we advance, the more successes we have, then the more wrathful will become the remnants of the defeated exploiting classes, the more quickly they turn to sharper forms of struggle, the more damage they do the Soviet state, the more they seize upon the most desperate means of struggle as the last resort of the doomed. . . .

8. It is necessary to smash and throw out another rotten theory which states that a person who does not always wreck things and who sometimes, if you please, is successful cannot be a wrecker.

This strange theory shows the naïveté of its authors. Not a single wrecker wrecks things all the time, if he does not wish to be exposed in the shortest possible time. On the contrary, contemporary wreckers must from time to time show successes in their work. . . .

9. It is necessary to smash and throw out a third rotten theory, which states that the systematic fulfillment of economic plans must nullify wrecking and the results of wrecking. . . .

10. It is necessary to smash and throw out a fourth rotten theory, which states that the Stakhanovite movement [to develop outstandingly efficient workers—*ed.*] is supposedly a basic means for struggle against wrecking. . . .

11. It is necessary to smash and throw out a fifth rotten theory, which states that the Trotskyist wreckers supposedly have no more reserves, that they have supposedly come to their last cadres. . . .

12. Finally, it is necessary to smash and throw out one more rotten theory, which states that, while we Bolsheviks are many and the wreck-

ers few, while tens of millions of people support us Bolsheviks and only individuals or tens the Trotskyist wreckers, it is perhaps unnecessary for we Bolsheviks to turn our attention to some handful of wreckers. . . .

Such are the measures that are necessary to liquidate these deficiencies. . . .

REPORT TO THE EIGHTEENTH
PARTY CONGRESS

From the closing years of the Thirties until the end of his life, Stalin was obliged to devote a substantial share of his attention to problems of international affairs. The Munich settlement of the Czech question in 1938 probably demonstrated to Stalin—who was not represented at the meeting—the dangers of entrusting the security of the USSR to alliance with France, the advocacy of "collective security" in the League of Nations, and the policy of a "united front" between non-Soviet Communist parties and the socialist parties. Perceiving the world through Leninist spectacles, his explanation of the failure of such defensive tactics emphasized two variables that seem to have dominated Stalin's approach to world affairs: (1) the intensity of the inevitable rivalry among the imperialist powers; (2) the intensity of the inevitable contradictions between capitalism and communism.

In his major address to the Eighteenth Party Congress in March, 1939—the last of his reports from the Central Committee to a congress—Stalin pretty clearly implied that he hoped that the intra-imperialist rivalries would be more intense than the capitalist-Communist contradictions in the immediate future, in order to permit the continued economic advance of the USSR, to which he devoted much attention elsewhere in the report. But the speech attempted more than a description of the world situation. It also conveyed a veiled warning to the Western democracies that Stalin did not intend to remain inactive while Britain and France encouraged Hitler to attack the USSR. And it conveyed a hint to Hitler that the USSR was not irrevocably determined to oppose Nazi expansion at the expense of other countries. The possible fiasco of Anglo-French policy, to which Stalin alludes at the end of the following excerpt, became all too real on August 23, 1939, when the Nazi-Soviet pact was signed—an attempt by Stalin to ensure that intra-imperialist conflicts would take precedence in Europe.

War is inexorable. It cannot be hidden under any guise. For no "axis pacts," "triangles," or "anti-Comintern pacts" can hide the fact that in

From "Report to the Eighteenth Party Congress." Stalin, *Problems of Leninism*, pp. 746-803.

this [recent] period Japan has seized a vast stretch of territory in China, that Italy has seized Abyssinia, that Germany has seized Austria and the Sudeten region, that Germany and Italy together have seized Spain— and all this in defiance of the interests of the nonaggressive states. The war remains a war; the military bloc of aggressors remains a military bloc; and the aggressors remain aggressors.

It is a distinguishing feature of the new imperialist war that it has not yet become universal, a world war. The war is being waged by aggressor states, who in every way infringe upon the interests of the nonaggressive states, primarily Britain, France, and the U.S.A., while the latter draw back and retreat, making concession after concession to the aggressors.

Thus we are witnessing an open redivision of the world and spheres of influence at the expense of the nonaggressive states, without the least attempt at resistance, and even with a certain connivance, on their part.

Incredible, but true.

To what are we to attribute this one-sided and strange character of the new imperialist war?

How is it that the nonaggressive countries, which possess such vast opportunities, have so easily and without resistance abandoned their positions and their obligations to please the aggressors?

Is it to be attributed to the weakness of the nonaggressive states? Of course not! Combined, the nonaggressive, democratic states are unquestionably stronger than the fascist states, economically and militarily.

To what then are we to attribute the systematic concessions made by these states to the aggressors?

It might be attributed, for example, to the fear that a revolution might break out if the nonaggressive states were to go to war and the war were to assume world-wide proportions. The bourgeois politicians know, of course, that the first imperialist world war led to the victory of the revolution in one of the largest countries. They are afraid that a second imperialist world war may also lead to victory of the revolution in one or several countries.

But at present this is not the sole or even the chief reason. The chief reason is that the majority of the nonaggressive countries, particularly Britain and France, have rejected the policy of collective security, the policy of collective resistance to aggressors, and have taken up a position of nonintervention, a position of "neutrality."

Formally speaking, the policy of nonintervention might be defined as follows: "Let each country defend itself against the aggressors as it likes and as best it can. That is not our affair. We shall trade both with the aggressors and with their victims." But actually speaking, the policy of nonintervention reveals an eagerness, a desire, not to hinder the aggressors in their nefarious work: not to hinder Japan, say, from embroiling herself in a war with China, or, better still, with the Soviet Union; not to hinder Germany, say, from enmeshing herself in European affairs, from embroiling herself in a war with the Soviet Union; [their policy reveals an eagerness] to allow all the belligerents to sink deeply into the mire of war, to encourage them to weaken and exhaust one another; and then, when they have become weak enough, to appear on the scene with fresh strength, to appear, of course, "in the interest of peace," and to dictate conditions to the enfeebled belligerents.

Cheap and easy. . . .

. . . take Germany, for instance. They let her have Austria, despite the undertaking to defend her independence; they let her have the Sudeten region; they abandoned Czechoslovakia to her fate, thereby violating all their obligations; and then they began to lie vociferously in the press about "the weakness of the Russian army," "the demoralization of the Russian air force," and "riots" in the Soviet Union, egging on the Germans to march farther east, promising them easy pickings, and prompting them: "Just start war on the Bolsheviks, and everything will be all right." It must be admitted that this too looks very much like egging on and encouraging the aggressor. . . .

Far be it from me to moralize on the policy of nonintervention, to talk of treason, treachery, and so on. It would be naïve to preach morals to people who recognize no human morality. Politics are politics, as the old, case-hardened bourgeois diplomats say. It must be remarked, however, that the big and dangerous political game started by the supporters of the policy of nonintervention may end in a serious fiasco for them.

Such is the true face of the now prevailing policy of nonintervention.

Such is the political situation in the capitalist countries.

THE TWENTY-SEVENTH
ANNIVERSARY OF THE
OCTOBER REVOLUTION

With the coming of the Second World War there were many changes in Stalin's public image. The civilian secretary general of the party, who had not held high office in the state (Soviet) structure since 1924, became Premier (Chairman of the Council of People's Commissars), Commissar of Defense, and Marshal of the Soviet Union (later Generalissimo). He also changed the tenor of his public pronouncements quite markedly; in his speech on the twenty-seventh anniversary of the proletarian revolution and in other statements Stalin seemed to indicate a real rapprochement with the Anglo-American bastions of capitalism. In harmony with this Stalin's appeals to the loyalty of his own populace were couched much more in terms of Russian patriotism than Communist doctrine.

Such statements are quite definitely misleading as a revelation of Stalin's sincere beliefs concerning his wartime allies, as we know now from the publication of such evidence as his snarling insinuation in 1945 that an Anglo-American attempt to secure the separate surrender of German forces in Italy was really a conspiracy with the Nazis against Russia. But to say that Stalin was at all times acutely suspicious of his allies and anxious to secure a strong postwar position for Soviet Russia is not to explain his specific ideas about the postwar world and the development of his strategy. Did Stalin ever intend to give the USSR a breathing-space for recovery and development by cooperating with his allies for a considerable time after the war? Or did he decide long before the defeat of Germany that he would soon bend every effort to spread communism from Canton to Calais? Or did Stalin follow some vacillating or intermediate line? There is still no firm evidence to provide a solution to this puzzle, and the following excerpt from Stalin's speech of November 6, 1944, might well be read simply as a reminder of the difficult problem that Stalin posed for Western policy-makers during the Second World War.

Like the immortal deeds of bravery of our soldiers at the front, the labor exploits of the Soviet people in the rear are rooted in the ardent, life-giving spirit of Soviet patriotism. The strength of Soviet patriotism is based on it, depending not on racial or nationalistic prejudice but on the people's profound devotion and loyalty to their Soviet homeland, on the fraternal partnership of the toiling people of all the nationalities of our country.

Soviet patriotism harmoniously blends the national traditions of the peoples and the common vital interests of all the toiling peoples of the Soviet Union. Far from dividing the nations and the peoples of our country, Soviet patriotism welds all of them into one fraternal family. This should be regarded as the basis of the inviolable and ever-stronger friendship among the peoples of the Soviet Union.

Moreover, the peoples of the USSR respect the rights and independence of the peoples of foreign countries and have always shown that they are willing to live in peace and friendship with their neighbor states. This should be regarded as the basis of the increasingly strong bonds between our state and the freedom-loving peoples. The reason Soviet men and women hate the German invaders is not that they are of different nationality, but that they have brought untold calamity and suffering on our people and on all freedom-loving peoples. It is an old saying of our people that the wolf is not beaten for being gray but for eating sheep.

The German fascists chose the misanthropic theory of race for their ideological weapon, expecting that by preaching bestial nationalism they would obtain the moral and political conditions for the German invaders' hegemony over the subjugated nations. In reality, however, the policy of racial hatred pursued by the Hitlerites has proved to be a source of internal weakness and international isolation to the German fascist state. . . .

The past year has been one of triumph for the common cause of the anti-German coalition, which has joined the peoples of the Soviet Union, Great Britain, and the United States in a fighting alliance. It has been a year of consolidation of their actions against Hitler Germany.

The decision of the Teheran Conference on joint measures against Germany and the brilliant execution of that decision is one of the striking proofs of the consolidation of the anti-Hitler coalition. There are few instances in history of plans for large-scale military operations undertaken in coalition against a common enemy which have been executed so completely and with such precision as the plan drawn up at the Teheran Conference for a joint blow against Germany. There can be no doubt that without unity of views and coordination of actions between

From "The Twenty-seventh Anniversary of the October Revolution." *Pravda*, November 7, 1944. Editor's translation.

the three great powers, the Teheran decision could not have been executed so fully and with such precision. Nor can there be any doubt that the successful realization of the Teheran decision was bound to enhance the consolidation of the United Nations front.

An equally striking indication of the solidity of the United Nations front is to be seen in the decisions of the Dumbarton Oaks Conference on postwar security [specifically on the future structure of the United Nations—*ed.*]. There is talk of disagreements between the three powers on certain security problems. Disagreements do exist, of course, and they will arise on a number of other issues as well. Disagreements may be found even among people in one and the same party. They are still more bound to occur between representatives of different states and different parties.

The surprising thing is not that disagreements occur but that there are so few of them and that in almost every case they are resolved in a spirit of unity and coordination among the three great powers.

What matters is not that there are disagreements but that these disagreements do not exceed the limits permitted by the interests of unity of the three great powers and that in the long run the disagreements are resolved in a spirit of full accord.

After her defeat Germany will of course be disarmed in both the economic and the military-political sense. But it would be naïve to think that she will not attempt to restore her power and launch new aggression. It is common knowledge that the German leaders are even now preparing for a new war. History demonstrates that a short period, about twenty or thirty years, is enough for Germany to recover from defeat and reestablish her power.

What are the means to prevent new German aggression, or to nip it in the bud and allow it no chance to grow into a great war, if it should somehow begin? . . .

There is only one means to this end, apart from the complete disarmament of the aggressive nations: that is, to establish a special organization composed of representatives of the peace-loving nations to maintain peace and safeguard security; to put at the disposal of the executive body of this organization at least the armed forces needed to avert aggression; and to oblige this organization to employ these armed forces without delay if it becomes necessary to avert or halt aggression and punish the guilty ones.

This must not be a repetition of the ill-fated League of Nations, which had neither the right nor the means to avert aggression. It will be a new, special, full empowered world organization, commanding all that is needed to maintain peace and avert new aggression.

Can we expect the actions of this world organization to be effective enough? They will be effective if the great powers which have borne the brunt of the war against Hitler continue to act in a spirit of unanimity and accord. They will not be effective if this essential condition is violated.

INTERVIEW ON CHURCHILL'S
"IRON CURTAIN" SPEECH

By the end of the war in 1945 it was clear that Stalin intended to maintain Soviet dominance in most of the East European territory that its troops occupied, regardless of promises of free elections. In a major speech of February, 1946, Stalin reminded his listeners that the essential difference between communism and capitalism remained in spite of wartime alliances. Amid widespread disbelief that Stalin would abandon collaboration with the other great powers, Churchill, then the ex-Prime Minister of Great Britain, declared before an audience in Fulton, Missouri, that the West should take a stand against the new Communist "Iron Curtain" that cuts across Europe from Stettin to Trieste.

Stalin replied in an "interview" with the official party newspaper in which he took the two-sided line that Soviet regime has followed since that time: the Soviet Union is committed to the existence of contradiction between communism and capitalism; nevertheless the Soviet Union is attempting to maintain peace, even in the face of aggressive provocation. In this way a policy of "peaceful co-existence" (without that particular slogan in 1946) was maintained while a far-reaching political offensive was being executed. While Stalin did not heap abuse on the United States as a nation in 1946, his spokesmen were undertaking a specifically anti-American program. During 1947, the year of the Marshall Plan and Truman Doctrine, this campaign swelled and it reached its peak during the Korean War of 1950-1953 with its charges of "germ warfare." The following excerpt from Stalin's attack on Churchill therefore does not convey the flavor of the cold war in full tilt. But it does point out the direction of the main line of postwar Soviet propaganda on world affairs: Communist expansion is pacific; capitalist resistance is aggressive.

Q. What is your appraisal of Mr. Churchill's recent speech in the United States of America?

From "Interview of Comrade J. V. Stalin with a *Pravda* Correspondent with Reference to Mr. Churchill's Speech." *Pravda*, March 14, 1946. Editor's translation.

A. I appraise it as a dangerous act, calculated to sow the seeds of discord among the allied states and to cause difficulty to their collaboration.

Q. May one consider that Mr. Churchill's speech has caused harm to the cause of peace and security?

A. Certainly. The essence of the affair is that Mr. Churchill now assumes the position of a warmonger. And Mr. Churchill is not alone in this; he has friends not only in England but also in the United States of America.

It should be noted that Mr. Churchill and his friends strikingly recall in this respect Hitler and his friends. Hitler began the task of unleashing war by proclaiming the racial theory, declaring that only people who spoke the German language constituted a full-fledged nation. Mr. Churchill, too, has begun the task of unleashing war with a racial theory, stating that only nations that speak the English language are full-fledged nations that are called upon to rule the destinies of the whole world. The German racial theory led Hitler and his friends to the point where the Germans, as the only full-fledged nation, were supposed to dominate other nations. The English racial theory leads Mr. Churchill and his friends to the conclusion that the English-speaking nations, as the only full-fledged ones, should dominate the rest of the nations of the world.

In essence Mr. Churchill and his friends in England and the U.S.A. have presented the non-English-speaking nations with something like an ultimatum: recognize our dominance voluntarily and then all will be in order; in the contrary case, war is inevitable.

But nations have shed their blood in the course of five years of cruel war for the freedom and independence of their countries and not to exchange domination by Hitler for domination by Churchill. It is wholly probable, therefore, that the non-English-speaking nations, which include the great majority of the population of the world, will not agree to accept a new slavery.

Mr. Churchill's tragedy is that he, as an inveterate Tory, does not understand this simple and obvious truth.

There is no doubt that Mr. Churchill's posture is the posture of war, an appeal to war with the USSR. . . .

Q. How do you appraise the part of Mr. Churchill's speech in which he attacks the democratic order in the European states that are our neighbors and in which he criticizes the good-neighborly relations that have been established between these nations and the Soviet Union?

A. This part of Mr. Churchill's speech is a mixture of elements of slander and elements of crudity and tactlessness.

Mr. Churchill declares that "Warsaw, Berlin, Prague, Vienna, Buda-

pest, Belgrade, Bucharest, Sofia—all these famous cities and the pop-
ulations of the surrounding region are in the Soviet sphere and all
are subjected in this or that form not only to Soviet influence but also
to a significant degree to the increasing control of Moscow." Mr.
Churchill characterizes all this as the boundless "expansionist tendencies" of the Soviet Union.

It does not require much effort to show that here Mr. Churchill
crudely and impudently slanders both Moscow and the aforemen-
tioned states that are neighbors of the USSR.

In the first place, it is completely absurd to speak of exclusive control by the USSR in Vienna and Berlin, where there are Allied Control Councils composed of representatives of four states and where
the USSR has only one-quarter of the votes. . . .

In the second place, one must not forget the following circumstances. The Germans launched the invasion of the USSR through
Finland, Poland, Rumania, Bulgaria, and Hungary. The Germans
were able to launch the invasion through these countries because in
these countries there were then governments that were hostile to the
USSR. As the result of the German invasion the Soviet Union has
lost about seven million persons forever in battle with the Germans
and, also thanks to German occupation, [in] the carrying off of Soviet
people into German forced labor. Needless to say, the Soviet Union
lost several times more people than England and the United States
of America put together. Possibly there is an inclination in some
places to consign to oblivion these colossal sacrifices of the Soviet
people, which secured the liberation of Europe from the Hitler yoke.
But the Soviet Union cannot forget them. It may be asked what can
be surprising about the Soviet Union wanting security in the future,
about its attempts to see to it that in these countries there are governments that have loyal relations with he Soviet Union? Is it possible, without taking leave of one's senses, to characterize these
peaceful efforts of the Soviet Union as expansionist tendencies of
our state? . . .

Mr. Churchill further declares that "the Communist parties which
were very insignificant in all these Eastern states of Europe have
gained exclusive power. . . ."

As is known, England is now governed by a government of one
party, the Laborists, by which the other parties are deprived of the
right to take part in the government of England. Mr. Churchill calls
this authentic democratism. Poland, Rumania, Yugoslavia, Bulguria,
Hungary are governed by a bloc of several parties—from four to six
parties—by which the opposition, if it is more or less loyal, secures
the right to take part in the government. Mr. Churchill calls this
totalitarianism, tyranny, a police-state. . . .

Mr. Churchill wants Poland to be governed by Sosnkowski and

Anders, Yugoslavia by Mikhailovich and Pavelich, Rumania by Prince Stirbey and Radescu [all non-Communists; Pavelich was a Croatian Nazi—*ed.*], Hungary and Austria by some king or other from the house of Habsburg and so on. Mr. Churchill wants to assure us that these gentlemen from the fascist hide-outs can secure "full democratism." Such is Mr. Churchill's "democratism."

Mr. Churchill strays near the truth when he speaks of the growth of the influence of Communist Parties in East Europe. One must note, however, that he is not entirely precise. The influence of the Communist Parties is growing not only in Eastern Europe but in almost all the countries of Europe in which fascism formerly held sway (Italy, Germany, Hungary, Bulgaria, Rumania, Finland) or where there was German or Italian occupation (France, Belgium, Holland, Norway, Denmark, Poland, Czechoslovakia, Yugoslavia, Greece, the Soviet Union, and so on).

The growth of the influence of the Communist Parties cannot be considered accidental. It is a completely regular phenomenon. The influence of the Communist Parties is growing because in the worst years of fascist domination in Europe the Communists seemed to be trustworthy, brave, self-sacrificing fighters against the fascist régime, for the freedom of the people. . . .

Such are the laws of historical development.

Of course, Mr. Churchill does not like such a development of events, and he frantically sounds the alarm, the call to arms. . . . I do not know if Mr. Churchill and his friends will succeed after the Second World War in organizing a new military campaign against "East Europe." But if they do succeed, which is unlikely since millions of "simple people" stand on guard in the cause of peace, then one may say with certainty that they will be beaten as they were beaten in the past [in the Russian Civil War—*ed.*], twenty-six years ago.

STALIN ON STALIN

From 1930 until 1953 the glorification of Stalin was one of the most salient features of Stalinist Communism. No excerpt can do justice to the immensity of this campaign, for its very soul was numbing redundancy. Nor can words alone do justice to the tragicomic spirit of a widely published photograph of a large number of beaming Soviet sailors treading water and bearing aloft pictures and slogans in praise of the chief.

To all appearances Stalin himself maintained an incongruous air of personal modesty that impressed a number of foreign visitors, and on one occasion he even issued a sharp rebuke to a colonel who had praised the leader in an article on military science (all other military writers did this, but Stalin chanced to write a published critique of this unfortunate colonel's work). Unlike Hitler, who explicitly supported the "leadership principle," Stalin in his theoretical "classic," "Dialectical and Historical Materialism," adhered to the Marxian tradition of historical determinism beyond the control of heroes.

However, no collection of Stalin's writings can afford entirely to ignore the whole literature of "the cult of the individual," as Khrushchev called it after Stalin was safely dead. And according to Khrushchev one need not go appreciably beyond the writings of **Stalin** himself to find a prime example of the literature of the cult. According to Khrushchev's speech of February 24-25, 1956, Stalin himself edited and considerably improved upon the text of the most widely circulated of all hosannahs to the leader: *Joseph Stalin: A Short Biography*. This small book was first published in 1939 and was republished in 1947 with appropriate coverage of Stalin's fresh glories. If Khrushchev is correct in stating that Stalin worked over the text, then it can be safely asserted that the following excerpt (the coda of a symphony of praise) is as much Stalin's personal handiwork as many of his major speeches and articles.

J. V. Stalin is the genius, the leader and teacher of the party, the great strategist of socialist revolution, helmsman of the Soviet state and cap-

From G. F. Alexandrov *et al.*, *Joseph Stalin: A Short Biography* (Moscow: Foreign Languages Publishing House, 1950).

tain of armies. An implacable attitude towards the enemies of socialism, profound fidelity to principle, a combination of clear revolutionary perspective and clarity of purpose with extraordinary firmness and persistence in the pursuit of aims, wise and practical leadership, and constant contact with the masses—such are the characteristic features of Stalin's style. After Lenin, no other leader in the world has been called upon to direct such vast masses of workers and peasants as J. V. Stalin. He has a unique faculty for generalizing the creative revolutionary experience of the masses, for seizing upon and developing their initiative, for learning from the masses as well as teaching them, and for leading them forward to victory.

Stalin's whole work is an example of profound theoretical power combined with an unusual breadth and versatility of practical experience in the revolutionary struggle.

In conjunction with the tried and tested Leninists who are his immediate associates, and at the head of the great Bolshevik Party, Stalin guides the destinies of a multinational socialist state, a state of workers and peasants of which there is no precedent in history. His advice is a guide to action in all fields of socialist construction. His work is extraordinary for its variety; his energy truly amazing. The range of questions which engage his attention is immense, embracing the most complex problems of Marxist-Leninist theory and school textbooks; problems of Soviet foreign policy and the municipal affairs of the proletarian capital; the development of the Great Northern Sea Route and the reclamation of the Colchian marshes; the advancement of Soviet literature and art and the editing of the model rules for collective farms; and, lastly, the solution of most intricate problems in the theory and practice of war.

Everybody is familiar with the cogent and invincible force of Stalin's logic, the crystal clarity of his mind, his iron will, his devotion to the party, his ardent faith in the people, and love for the people. Everybody is familiar with his modesty, his simplicity of manner, his consideration for people, and his merciless severity towards enemies of the people. Everybody is familiar with his intolerance of ostentation, of phrasemongers and windbags, of whiners and alarmists. Stalin is wise and deliberate in solving complex political questions where a thorough weighing of pros and cons is required. At the same time, he is a supreme master of bold revolutionary decisions and of swift realignments.

Stalin is the worthy continuer of the cause of Lenin, or, as it is said in the party: Stalin is the Lenin of today.

Replying to the congratulations of public bodies and individuals on his fiftieth birthday, in 1929, Stalin wrote: "I set down your congratulations and greetings as addressed to the great party of the working class, which begot me and reared me in its image. . . .

"You need have no doubt, comrades, that I am prepared in the future, too, to devote to the cause of the working class, to the cause of the proletarian revolution and world communism, all my strength, all my faculties, and, if need be, all my blood, to the very last drop."

In the eyes of the peoples of the USSR., Stalin is the incarnation of their heroism, their love of their country, their patriotism. "For Stalin! For our country!"—it was with this cry that the valiant Soviet Army demolished its malignant and treacherous enemy, fascist Germany, and hoisted the flag of victory over Berlin.

"For Stalin! For our country!"—it was with this cry that the men of the Soviet Army and Navy demolished imperialist Japan and brought security to the frontiers of the Soviet Union in the Far East.

With the name of Stalin in their hearts, the working class of the Soviet Union performed unparalleled feats of labor in the Great Patriotic War, supplying the Red Army with first-class weapons and ammunition.

With the name of Stalin in their hearts, the collective farmers toiled devotedly in the fields to supply the Red Army and the cities with food, and industry with raw materials.

With the name of Stalin in their hearts, the Soviet intelligentsia worked with might and main in defence of their country, perfecting the weapons of the Red Army and the technique and organization of industry, and furthering Soviet science and culture.

With the name of Stalin in their hearts, the entire Soviet people are now successfully repairing the damage caused by the war and are striving for a new powerful advance of the Soviet national economy and Soviet culture.

Stalin's name is a symbol of the courage and glory of the Soviet people, a call to heroic deeds for the welfare of their great Motherland.

Stalin's name is cherished by the boys and girls of the socialist land, by the Young Pioneers. Their dearest ambition is to be like Lenin and Stalin, to be political figures of the Lenin and Stalin type. At the call of the party and Comrade Stalin, the youth of the Soviet Union have erected giant socialist industrial plants, have reared cities in the taiga, have built splendid ships, are conquering the Arctic, are mastering new methods in industry and agriculture, are strengthening the defences of our Motherland, are working creatively in the sciences and the arts. At the call of the party and Stalin, they displayed exemplary heroism and courage in the battlefields of the Patriotic War and exemplary devotion in the rear, working for the victory of the Red Army. Fostered by Lenin and Stalin, the Young Communist League is a true aid of the Bolshevik Party, a reliable successor to the older generation of fighters for communism.

In all their many languages the peoples of the Soviet Union compose songs to Stalin, expressing their supreme love and boundless devotion for their great leader, teacher, friend, and military commander.

In the lore and art of the people, Stalin's name is ever linked with Lenin's. "We go with Stalin as with Lenin, we talk to Stalin as to Lenin;

he knows all our inmost thoughts; all his life he has cared for us," runs one of the many exquisite Russian folk tales of today.

The name of Stalin is a symbol of the moral and political unity of Soviet society.

With the name of Stalin, all progressive men and women, all the freedom-loving democratic peoples associate their hope for lasting peace and security.

"It is our good fortune that in the trying years of the war the Red Army and the Soviet people were led forward by the wise and tested leader of the Soviet Union—the Great Stalin. With the name of Generalissimo Stalin the glorious victories of our army will go down in the history of our country and in the history of the world. Under the guidance of Stalin, the great leader and organizer, we are now proceeding to peaceful constructive labors, striving to bring the forces of socialist society to full fruition and to justify the dearest hopes of our friends all over the world." *

* V. M. Molotov, *Speech on the 29th Anniversary of the Great October Socialist Revolution,* Russ. ed., 1945, pp. 18-19.

LETTER TO THE YUGOSLAV
COMMUNISTS

Considering the importance that Stalin attached to theory in his most widely published works, it is strange indeed that he (and his lieutenants) had so little to say about the theoretical problems associated with the appearance of a variety of new Communist-dominated states in the years 1946-1949. It is true that a theory of "people's democracy" emerged in East Europe with Stalin's tacit approval, but on balance the alleged genius of Marxism-Leninism seemed remarkably tongue-tied. In part this may have been a reflection of the weariness of years and of genuine puzzlement by the new development. But it is also probable that Stalin's desire not to alarm the West more than necessary concerning developments in East Europe played a major part in inhibiting public doctrinal statements on such touchy matters as the degree of subordination of satellites to Moscow. While Soviet publicity maintained that the European satellites were wholly sovereign, it is pretty clear that Stalin did not want to communicate such notions to Communist leaders in the area.

At least some idea of Stalin's ideas on the new Communist realm in Europe can be gained from documents published as a result of Stalin's most notable failure in East Europe, the Soviet-Yugoslav dispute of 1948. The Communist Party of Yugoslav (CPY), led by Tito, came to power without much Soviet assistance and without military occupation, unlike most satellite governments. The proud Yugoslav Communists, while bursting with pro-Soviet spirits, expected to be able to count on Soviet help while charting their own path to utopia, and when they found Moscow more generous with condescending advice and surveillance than with aid, Tito and his colleagues objected. Following an exchange of sharp letters in the spring of 1948, the Soviets and their East European publicity organ, the Communist Information Bureau, read the Yugoslav Party out of the Marxist-Leninist faith. Stalin erroneously expected the shock to unseat Tito and permit the reorganization of Yugoslav communism on more acceptable lines.

The following excerpt is from a letter of May 4, 1948, from the Central Committee of the Communist Party of the Soviet Union to the Yugoslav Communists. Although not signed by Stalin, it could only have been sent with his personal approval, and it is about the best available guide to his conception of subordination of satellites to Moscow in the postwar empire. It was subsequently published by the Tito government that amazed the world with its defiance. Unfortunately, the only published letters from Stalin (or the Central Committee) to the most important of the new Communist states, China, are less informative pleasantries.

For the information of Comrades Tito and Kardelj, it is necessary to mention that, unlike the Yugoslavs, we do not consider the Yugoslav Ambassador in Moscow as a mere official; we do not treat him as a mere bourgeois ambassador and we do not deny this "right to seek information about the work of our party from anyone he chooses." Because he became an ambassador, he did not stop being a Communist. We consider him as a comrade and high-ranking Communist. He has friends and acquaintances among the Soviet people. Is he "acquiring" information about the work of our party? Most likely he is. Let him "acquire" it. We have no reason to hide from comrades the shortcomings in our party. We expose them ourselves in order to eliminate them.

We consider that this attitude of the Yugoslav comrades towards the Soviet Ambassador cannot be regarded as accidental. It arises from the general attitude of the Yugoslav government, which is also the cause of the inability of the Yugoslav leaders to see the difference between the foreign policy of the USSR and the foreign policy of the Anglo-Americans; they, therefore, put the foreign policy of the USSR on a par with the foreign policy of the English and Americans and feel that they should follow the same policy towards the Soviet Union as towards the imperialist states, Great Britain and the United States. . . .

In our letter we wrote that the spirit of the policy of class struggle is not felt in the CPY, that the capitalist elements are increasing in the cities and the villages and that the leaders of the Party are not undertaking any measures to check the capitalist elements.

Comrades Tito and Kardelj deny all this and consider our statements, which are a matter of principle, as insults to the CPY, avoiding an answer to the essential question. Their proofs are based only on the fact that consistent social reforms are being undertaken in Yugoslavia. However, this is almost negligible. The denial on the part of these comrades of the strengthening of the capitalist elements and, in connection with this, the sharpening of the class struggle in the village under the conditions of contemporary Yugoslavia arise from the opportunist contention that, in the

Originally titled "Letter of 4 May 1948 from the CPSU to the CPY." This selection is taken from *The Soviet-Yugoslav Dispute* published by the Oxford University Press under the auspices of the Royal Institute of International Affairs. Reprinted by permission of the Oxford University Press.

transition period between capitalism and socialism, the class struggle does not become sharper, as taught by Marxism-Leninism, but dies out, as averred by opportunists of the type of Bukharin, who postulated a decadent theory of the peaceful absorption of the capitalist elements into the socialist structure.

No one will deny that the social reforms which occurred in the USSR after the October Revolution were all-embracing and consistent with our teaching. However, this did not cause the CPSU [Communist Party of the Soviet Union—*ed.*] to conclude that the class struggle in our country was weakening, nor that there was no danger of the strengthening of the capitalist elements. In 1920-21 Lenin stated that "while we live in a country of smallholders there is a stronger economic basis for capitalism in Russia than there is for communism," since "small-scale individual farming gives birth to capitalism and the bourgeoisie continually, daily, hourly, spontaneously and on a mass scale." It is known that for fifteen years after the October Revolution, the question of measures for checking capitalist class was never taken off the daily agenda of our Party. To underestimate the experiences of the CPSU in matters relating to the development of socialism in Yugoslavia is a great political danger, and cannot be allowed for Marxists, because socialism cannot be developed only in the cities, and in industry, but must also be developed in the villages and in agriculture.

It is no accident that the leaders of the CPY are avoiding the question of the class struggle and the checking of the capitalist elements in the village. What is more, in the speeches of the Yugoslav leaders there is no mention of the question of class differentiation in the village; the peasantry are considered as an organic whole, and the party does not mobilize its forces in an effort to overcome the difficulties arising from the increase of the exploiting elements in the village.

However, the political situation in the village gives no cause for complacency. Where, as in Yugoslavia, there is no nationalization of the land, where private ownership of the land exists and land is bought and sold, where considerable portions of land are concentrated in the hands of the kulaks, where hired labour is used, etc. the party cannot be educated in the spirit of camouflaging the class struggle and smoothing over class controversies without disarming itself for the struggle with the main difficulties in the development of socialism. This means that the CPY is being lulled to sleep by the decadent opportunist theory of the peaceful infiltration of capitalist elements into socialism, borrowed from Bernstein, Vollmar ["revisionists"—*ed.*], and Bukharin.

Nor is it by accident that some of the most prominent leaders of the CPY are deviating from the Marxist-Leninist road on the question of the leading role of the working class. While Marxism-Leninism starts by recognizing the leading role of the working class in the process of liquidating capitalism and [of] developing a socialist society, the leaders of the CPY have an entirely different opinion. It is enough to quote the following speech by Comrade Tito in Zagreb on 2 November 1946: "We do not tell the peasants that they are the strongest pillar of our State in order that, eventually, we may get their votes, but because we know that that is what they are, and because they should be aware of what they are."

This attitude is in complete contradiction to Marxism-Leninism. Marxism-Leninism considers that in Europe and in the countries of people's democracy, the working class and not the peasantry is the most progressive, the most revolutionary class. As regards the peasantry, or rather its majority—the poor and middle peasants—they can be or are in a union with the working class, while the leading role in this union still belongs to the working class. However, the passage quoted not only denies the leading role to the working class, but proclaims that the entire peasantry, including . . . the kulaks, is the strongest pillar in the new Yugoslavia. As can be seen this attitude expresses opinions which are natural to petty-bourgeois politicians but not to Marxist-Leninists. . . .

Tito and Kardelj, in their letter, speak of the merits and successes of the CPY, saying that the Central Committee of the CPSU earlier acknowledged these services and successes, but it is now supposedly silent about them. This, naturally, is not true. No one can deny the services and successes of the CPY. There is no doubt about this. However, we must also say that the services of the Communist Parties of Poland, Czechoslovakia, Hungary, Rumania, Bulgaria, and Albania are not less than those of the CPY. However the leaders of these parties behave modestly and do not boast about their successes, as do the Yugoslav leaders, who have pierced everyone's ears by their unlimited self-praises. It is also necessary to emphasize that the services of the French and Italian CP's to the revolution were not less but greater than those of Yugoslavia. Even though the French and Italian CP's have so far achieved less success than the CPY, this is not due to any special qualities of the CPY, but mainly because after the destruction of the Yugoslav Partisan Headquarters by German paratroopers, at a moment when the people's liberation movement in Yugoslavia was passing through a serious crisis, the Soviet army came to the aid of the Yugoslav people, crushed the German invader, liberated Belgrade and in this way created the conditions which were necessary for the CPY to achieve power. Unfortunately the Soviet army did not and could not render such assistance to the French and Italian CP's. If Comrade Tito and Comrade Kardelj bore this fact in mind they would be less boastful about their merits and successes and would behave with greater propriety and modesty. . . .

ECONOMIC PROBLEMS OF
SOCIALISM IN THE USSR

In October, 1952, on the eve of the long-deferred Nineteenth Party Congress, Stalin published his last substantial doctrinal pronouncement. This was actually a collection of replies that Stalin addressed to various economists between February and September, 1952, brought together under the general title appearing above. Naturally the entire Soviet propaganda apparatus went into high gear to praise this rare contribution to scientific socialism.

Although this claim need not be taken seriously (even before Khrushchev's anti-Stalin campaign, Mikoyan had attacked "Economic Problems"), these last important writings of Stalin are of interest for the light they cast on his outlook on world affairs and the path to utopia. The first part of the following selection from his "Remarks on Economic Questions Connected with the November 1951 Discussion" (signed February 1, 1952) provides considerable insight on the combination of flexibility and stubbornness in Stalin's approach to international affairs. As much as ever he insists on the long-term necessity of overthrowing "imperialism"; on the other hand, the Soviet Union supports peace and does not consider war with the capitalists to be inevitable. In other words Stalin wished to retain flexibility to stiffen or soften his approach to the West as circumstances dictated. In publicly assuring the Soviet economists that war between the ideologies is not inevitable, Stalin was probably offering a cautious peace feeler to the forces engaged against him in Korea. On the other hand, it was still possible that the "fight for peace" may become a revolutionary struggle at any time. The old man, sometimes accused of rigidity, seems to have been conducting a highly flexible probing operation.

The second part of the excerpt, dated May 22, 1952, concerns not current affairs so much as the destiny of man. For one who insisted on great sacrifice to advance to the perfect society, Stalin had said very little about the character of this goal. In 1936 the new constitution reflected the completion of the way-station of "socialism," and by 1952 it was high time for some kind of progress report on the further progress of the country. This Stalin somewhat cryptically provided in this last doctrinal work by describing the conditions that had to be met to achieve "communism." How long the transition he described would be likely to take and what specific current policies were planned for this purpose, Stalin did not make very clear.

Some comrades hold that, owing to the development of new international conditions since the Second World War, wars between capitalist countries have ceased to be inevitable. They consider that the contradictions between the socialist camp and the capitalist camp are more acute than the contradictions among the capitalist countries; that the U.S.A. has brought the other capitalist countries sufficiently under its sway to be able to prevent their going to war among themselves and weakening one another; that the foremost capitalist minds have been sufficiently taught by the two world wars and the severe damage they caused to the whole capitalist world not to venture to involve the capitalist countries in war with one another again—and that, because of all this, wars between capitalist countries are no longer inevitable.

These comrades are mistaken. They see the outward phenomena that come and go on the surface, but they do not see those profound forces which, although they are so far operating imperceptibly, will nevertheless determine the course of developments.

Outwardly, everything would seem to be "going well": the U.S.A. has put Western Europe, Japan and other capitalist countries on rations; Germany (Western), Britain, France, Italy and Japan have fallen into the clutches of the U.S.A. and are meekly obeying its commands. But it would be mistaken to think that things can continue to "go well" for "all eternity," that these countries will tolerate the domination and oppression of the United States endlessly, that they will not endeavor to tear loose from American bondage and take the path of independent development.

Take, first of all, Britain and France. Undoubtedly, they are imperialist countries. Undoubtedly, cheap raw materials and secure markets are of paramount importance to them. Can it be assumed that they will endlessly tolerate the present situation, in which, under the guise of "Marshall Plan aid," Americans are penetrating into the economies of Britain and France and trying to convert them into adjuncts of the United States economy, and American capital is seizing raw materials and markets in the British and French colonies and thereby plotting disaster for the high profits of the British and French capitalists? Would it not be truer to say that capitalist Britain, and, after her, capitalist France, will be compelled in the end to break from the embrace of the U.S.A. and enter into conflict with it in order to secure an independent position and, of course, high profits?

From Stalin, *Economic Problems of Socialism in the U.S.S.R.* (Moscow: Foreign Languages Publishing House, 1952).

Let us pass to the major vanquished countries, Germany (Western) and Japan. These countries are now languishing in misery under the jackboot of American imperialism. Their industry and agriculture, their trade, their foreign and home policies, and their whole life are fettered by the American occupation "regime." Yet only yesterday these countries were great imperialist powers and were shaking the foundations of the domination of Britain, the U.S.A., and France in Europe and Asia. To think that these countries will not try to get on their feet again, will not try to smash the U.S. "regime" and force their way to independent development, is to believe in miracles.

It is said that the contradictions between capitalism and socialism are stronger than the contradictions among the capitalist countries. Theoretically, of course, that is true. It is not only true now, today; it was true before the Second World War. And it was more or less realized by the leaders of the capitalist countries. Yet the Second World War began not as a war with the USSR, but as a war between capitalist countries. Why? Firstly, because war with the USSR, as a socialist land, is more dangerous to capitalism than war between capitalist countries; for whereas war between capitalist countries puts in question only the supremacy of certain capitalist countries over others, war with the USSR must certainly put in question the existence of capitalism itself. Secondly, because the capitalists, although they clamor, for "propaganda" purposes, about the aggressiveness of the Soviet Union, do not themselves believe that it is aggressive, because they are aware of the Soviet Union's peaceful policy and know that it will not attack capitalist countries.

After the First World War it was similarly believed that Germany had been definitely put out of action, just as certain comrades now believe that Japan and Germany have been definitely put out of action. Then, too, it was said and clamored in the press that the United States had put Europe on rations, that Germany would never rise to her feet again, and that there would be no more wars between capitalist countries. In spite of this, Germany rose to her feet again as a great power within the space of some fifteen or twenty years after her defeat, having broken out of bondage and taken the path of independent development. And it is significant that it was none other than Britain and the United States that helped Germany to recover economically and to enhance her economic war potential. Of course, when the United States and Britain assisted Germany's economic recovery, they did so with a view to setting a recovered Germany against the Soviet Union, to utilizing her against the land of socialism. But Germany directed her forces in the first place against the Anglo-French-American bloc. And when Hitler Germany declared war on the Soviet Union, the Anglo-French-American bloc, far from joining with Hitler Germany, was compelled to enter into a coalition with the USSR against Hitler Germany.

Consequently, the struggle of the capitalist countries for markets and their desire to crush their competitors proved in practice to be stronger than the contradictions between the capitalist camp and the socialist camp.

What guarantee is there, then, that Germany and Japan will not rise to their feet again, will not attempt to break out of American bondage and live their own independent lives? I think there is no such guarantee.

But it follows from this that the inevitability of wars between capitalist countries remains in force.

It is said that Lenin's thesis that imperialism inevitably generates wars must now be regarded as obsolete, since powerful popular forces have come forward today in defence of peace and against another world war. That is not true.

The object of the present-day peace movement is to rouse the masses of the people to fight for the preservation of peace and for the prevention of another world war. Consequently, the aim of this movement is not to overthrow capitalism and establish socialism—it confines itself to the democratic aim of preserving peace. In this respect, the present-day peace movement differs from the movement of the time of the First World War for the conversion of the imperialist war into civil war, since the latter movement went farther and pursued socialist aims.

It is possible that in a definite conjuncture of circumstances the fight for peace will develop here or there into a fight for socialism. But then it will no longer be the present-day peace movement; it will be a movement for the overthrow of capitalism.

What is most likely is that the present-day peace movement, as a movement for the preservation of peace, will, if it succeeds, result in preventing a particular war, in its temporary postponement, in the temporary preservation of a particular peace, in the resignation of a bellicose government and its supersession by another that is prepared temporarily to keep the peace. That, of course, will be good. Even very good. But, all the same, it will not be enough to eliminate the inevitability of wars between capitalist countries generally. It will not be enough, because, for all the successes of the peace movement, imperialism will remain, continue in force—and, consequently, the inevitability of wars will also continue in force.

To eliminate the inevitability of war, it is necessary to abolish imperialism. . . .

In order to pave the way for a real, and not declaratory, transition to communism, at least three main preliminary conditions have to be satisfied.

1. It is necessary, in the first place, to ensure, not a mythical "rational organization" of the productive forces, but a continuous expansion of all social production, with a relatively higher rate of expansion of the production of means of production. The relatively higher rate of ex-

pansion and production of means of production is necessary not only because it has to provide the equipment both for its own plants and for all other branches of the national economy, but also because reproduction on an extended scale becomes altogether impossible without it.

2. It is necessary, in the second place, by means of gradual transitions carried out to the advantage of the collective farms, and, hence, of all society, to raise collective-farm property to the level of public property, and, also by means of gradual transitions, to replace commodity circulation by a system of products-exchange, under which the central government, or some other social-economic center, might control the whole product of social production in the interests of society.

Comrade Yaroshenko is mistaken when he asserts that there is no contradiction between the relations of production and the productive forces of society under socialism. Of course, our present relations of production are in a period when they fully conform to the growth of the productive forces and help to advance them at seven-league strides. But it would be wrong to rest easy at that and to think that there are no contradictions between our productive forces and the relations of production. There certainly are, and will be, contradictions, seeing that the development of the relations of production lags, and will lag, behind the development of the productive forces. Given a correct policy on the part of the directing bodies, these contradictions cannot grow into antagonisms, and there is no chance of matters coming to a conflict between the relations of production and the productive forces of society. It would be a different matter if we were to conduct a wrong policy, such as that which Comrade Yaroshenko recommends. In that case conflict would be inevitable, and our relations of production might become a serious brake on the further development of the productive forces.

The task of directing bodies is therefore promptly to discern incipient contradictions, and to take timely measures to resolve them by adapting the relations of production to the growth of the productive forces. This, above all, concerns such economic factors as group, or kolkhoz, property and commodity circulation. At present, of course, these factors are being successfully utilized by us for the promotion of the socialist economy, and they are of undeniable benefit to our society. It is undeniable, too, that they will be of benefit also in the near future. But it would be unpardonable blindness not to see at the same time that these factors are already beginning to hamper the powerful development of our productive forces, since they create obstacles to the full extension of government planning to the whole of the national economy, especially agriculture. There is no doubt that these factors will hamper the continued growth of the productive forces of our country more and more as time goes on. The task therefore is to eliminate these contradictions by gradually converting collective-farm property into public property, and by introducing—also gradually—products-exchange in place of commodity circulation.

3. It is necessary, in the third place, to ensure such a cultural advancement of society as will secure for all members of society the all-round development of their physical and mental abilities, so that the members of society may be in a position freely to choose their occupations and not be tied all their lives, owing to the existing division of labor, to some one occupation.

What is required for this?

It would be wrong to think that such a substantial advance in the cultural standard of the members of society can be brought about without substantial changes in the present status of labor. For this, it is necessary, first of all, to shorten the working day at least to six, and subsequently five hours. This is needed in order that the members of society might have the necessary, free time to receive an all-round education. It is necessary, further, to introduce universal compulsory polytechnical education, which is required in order that the members of society might be able freely to choose their occupations and not be tied to some one occupation all their lives. It is likewise necessary that housing conditions should be radically improved, and that real wages of workers and employees should at least be doubled, if not more, both by means of direct increases of wages and salaries, and, more especially, by further systematic reductions of prices for consumer goods.

These are the basic conditions required to pave the way for the transition to communism.

Only after all these preliminary conditions are satisfied in their entirety will it be possible to pass from the socialist formula, "from each according to his ability, to each according to his work," to the Communist formula, "from each according to his ability, to each according to his needs."

This will be a radical transition from one form of economy of socialism, to another, higher form of economy, the economy of communism. . . .

KHRUSHCHEV

KHRUSHCHEV ON THE
PURGE TRIALS

Although the following excerpt has no stature in the literature of Bolshevism, it is worth reading for comparison with Khrushchev's justly famous speech of 1956 against Stalin, which forms the second selection from Khrushchev's works. On January 30, 1937, when the following speech was delivered, Khrushchev was the secretary of the party committees for Moscow city and the surrounding region, a major responsibility. It was also a risky job because the purges of this time, including both highly publicized and strictly secret prosecutions, jeopardized the security of the leading party figures most of all. The trial of seventeen Bolsheviks on charges of treason, espionage, acts of diversion, wrecking, and the preparation of terrorist acts concluded on January 30 with death sentences for thirteen of the accused. As responsible party official for the crucial Moscow region, Khrushchev had to make sure that the judicial decision received wide and rapid dissemination and, as potential purgee, he had to show his zealous loyalty in joining the incantations against the "guilty."

Khrushchev met these needs by organizing an extraordinary mass demonstration of an estimated 200,000 Muscovites on Red Square, to whom he addressed the words that follow. In the light of his statements of 1956 regarding "the cult of the individual" and the purges, one can only wonder what was passing through his mind on January 30, 1937. In any case the speech was a success; Khrushchev did not fall victim to Stalin's police and was promoted the following year to the status of candidate member of the Politburo, the highest council of the party.

Comrade workers, men and women, engineers, employees, men of science and art, and all working people of our country! We are gathered here, on Red Square, to raise our proletarian voice in complete support of the sentence passed by the Military Collegium of the Supreme Court against the enemies of the people, the traitors of the motherland, the

"Khrushchev on the Purge Trials." From *Pravda*, January 31, 1937. Editor's translation.

betrayers of the workers' cause, the spies, the diversionists, agents of fascism, the vile, despicable Trotskyists.

Here on Red Square before all the peoples of the Soviet Land, before the workers of all the world, we approve this sentence and declare that any enemy who tries to stop our victorious advance to a Communist society will be crushed by us and annihilated! . . .

The Trotskyists fought the destruction of the achievements of the working class of the USSR, achievements that are recorded in the Stalin Constitution. They wanted to destroy the seven-hour working day, to destroy our great right to labor, rest, and education, to revive the great terror of unemployment, from which the workers of our country were delivered by the victory of socialism.

The Trotskyists wanted to dissolve the collective farms. The Trotskyist wretches dreamed that, as it was in tsarist Russia and as it is in the entire capitalist world, there would again arise in our countryside one extreme of impoverished and starving millions and on the other extreme rich groups of kulaks.

Judas Trotsky and his gang intended to betray the Ukraine, the Maritime, and the Amur regions to the German and Japanese imperialists and to transform our blooming motherland into a colony of German and Japanese imperialism.

They wanted to degrade the Russian, Ukrainian, White Russian, Georgian, and all other people of the USSR to the level of "inferior races," which would be ruled by the "super-race" of plundering German fascism. . . .

These assassins aimed at the heart and brain of our party. They raised their evil hand against Comrade Stalin. Raising their hand against Stalin, they raised it against all of us, against the laboring class, against the workers! Raising their hand against Comrade Stalin, they raised it against the teaching of Marx-Engels-Lenin!

Raising their hand against Comrade Stalin, they raised it against all that is best, all that is human, because Stalin is hope, aspiration, the beacon of all advanced and progressive humanity. Stalin is our banner! Stalin is our will! Stalin is our victory!

THE "SECRET" SPEECH TO THE
TWENTIETH PARTY CONGRESS

For nineteen years following his speech on Red Square against the alleged Trotskyists Khrushchev seemed to be a good Stalinist. While Stalin lived this was inevitable for any Soviet politician, but, even after the death of the old leader, Khrushchev seemed disinclined to break openly with the Stalinist tradition. Shortly before the Twentieth Party Congress convened in February, 1956, an organ of the party that was subject to Khrushchev's control announced the revival of publication of Stalin's *Works* after several years' interruption. And, in the open sessions of the Congress, Khrushchev presented the report of the Central Committee without any attack on Stalin, in contrast to the speech of another old Stalinist, Mikoyan, who did permit himself some explicit criticism of the deceased dictator.

But at about this time some considerations that are not yet clear impelled Khrushchev, the aspirant dictator, to launch a bitter and comprehensive assault on the reputation of the previous ruler. By Khrushchev's later—and scarcely disinterested—account, Molotov, Malenkov, and others strained every effort to stop him, but failed to break his will and dared not attempt physical coercion. Quite likely this struggle accounts for the delay in the delivery of the speech from the evening until midnight of February 24. And the attempt at secrecy during the session, including the exclusion of observers from foreign Communist Parties, may well have been a concession to "Stalinist" opposition. It now seems unlikely that Khrushchev was completely bent upon keeping the speech a secret, for copies of it were circulated on loan to a wide circle of party organizations in the USSR and to foreign Communist Parties not long after the Congress. Anyone with Khrushchev's experience in security problems would know that such dissemination, despite various safeguards, is most likely to lead to disclosures, as did in fact occur. After fairly accurate but incomplete versions of the speech had been reported by Reuters and by the Yugoslav Communists, the United States Department of State on June 4, 1956, released a more or less full version that had been covertly obtained from some non-Russian Communist Party.

This touched off a major furor in European and American Com-

munist circles, although the very existence of the "secret" session
was officially ignored in the Soviet Union. Thus the most important
document on Russian communism to appear in at least a generation
remained a semisecret, never mentioned in the Soviet press, until
the Twenty-second Party Congress in 1961. Some of the historical
documents to which Khrushchev referred were published in Russia
in June, 1956 (in the main they had been known to the outside
world for many years), and the press carried various less specific
and virulent attacks on Stalin. But only after Khrushchev had
worked mightily to dispose of almost all major leaders of the Stalin era did he publicly acknowledge that he had delivered the
secret speech, revealing a good part of its argument to an open session of the Twenty-second Congress and in the published record.
But an official version of the "secret" speech (or a wholly reliable
one, which is something else again) has yet to appear, and the following excerpts are from the State Department edition, slightly
modified in matters of English style.

Comrades! In the report of the Central Committee of the party at the
20th Congress, in a number of speeches by delegates to the Congress,
as also formerly during the plenary sessions of the Central Committee
of the Communist Party of the Soviet Union sessions, quite a lot has
been said about the cult of the individual and about its harmful consequences.

After Stalin's death the Central Committee of the party began to
implement a policy of explaining concisely and consistently that it is
impermissible and foreign to the spirit of Marxism-Leninism to elevate
one person, to transform him into a superman possessing supernatural
characteristics, akin to those of a god. Such a man supposedly knows
everything, sees everything, thinks for everyone, can do anything, is infallible in his behavior.

Such a belief about a man, and specifically about Stalin, was cultivated
among us for many years.

The objective of the present report is not a thorough evaluation of
Stalin's life and activity. Concerning Stalin's merits, an entirely sufficient
number of books, pamphlets, and studies had already been written in
his lifetime. The role of Stalin in the preparation and execution of the
Socialist Revolution, in the Civil War, and in the fight for the construction of socialism in our country is universally known. Everyone knows
this well.

At present, we are concerned with a question which has immense
importance for the party now and for the future—with how the cult of

"The 'Secret' Speech to the Twentieth Party Congress." From *The Congressional
Record*, June 4, 1956.

the person of Stalin has been gradually growing, the cult which became at a certain specific stage the source of a whole series of exceedingly serious and grave perversions of party principles, of party democracy, of revolutionary legality.

Because of the fact that not all as yet realize fully the practical consequences resulting from the cult of the individual, the great harm caused by the violation of the principle of collective direction of the party and because of the accumulation of immense and limitless power in the hands of one person, the Central Committee of the party considers it absolutely necessary to make the material pertaining to this matter available to the 20th Congress of the Communist Party of the Soviet Union. . . .

Facts prove that many abuses were made on Stalin's orders without taking into consideration any norms of party and Soviet legality. Stalin was a very distrustful man, sickly suspicious; we know this from our work with him. He could look at a man and say: "Why are your eyes so shifty today?" or "Why are you turning so much today and avoiding to look me directly in the eyes?" The sickly suspicion created in him a general distrust even toward eminent party workers whom he had known for years. Everywhere and in everything he saw "enemies," "two-facers," and "spies." Possessing unlimited power, he indulged in great willfulness and choked a person morally and physically. A situation was created where one could not express one's own will.

When Stalin said that one or another should be arrested, it was necessary to accept on faith that he was an "enemy of the people." Meanwhile, Beria's gang, which ran the organs of state security, outdid itself in proving the guilt of the arrested and the truth of materials which it falsified. And what proofs were offered? The confessions of the arrested, and the investigative judges accepted these "confessions." And how is it possible that a person confesses to crimes which he has not committed? Only in one way—because of application of physical methods of pressuring him, tortures, bringing him to a state of unconsciousness. deprivation of his judgment, taking away of his human dignity. In this manner were "confessions" acquired. . . .

Very grievous consequences, especially in reference to the beginning of the war, followed Stalin's annihilation of many military commanders and political workers during 1937-1941 because of his suspiciousness and through slanderous accusations. During these years repressions were instituted against certain parts of military cadres beginning literally at the company and battalion commander level and extending to the higher military centers; during this time the cadre of leaders who had gained military experience in Spain and in the Far East was almost completely liquidated.

The policy of large-scale repression against the military cadres led also to undermined military discipline, because for several years officers of all ranks and even soldiers in the party and Komsomol cells were taught to "unmask" their superiors as hidden enemies. (Movement in the hall.) It is natural that this caused a negative influence on the state of military discipline in the first period of the war. . . .

It would be incorrect to forget that, after the first severe disaster and defeat at the front, Stalin thought that this was the end. In one of his speeches in these days he said: "All that which Lenin created we have lost forever."

After this Stalin for a long time actually did not direct the military operations and ceased to do anything whatever. He returned to active leadership only when some members of the Politburo visited him and told him that it was necessary to take certain steps immediately in order to improve the situation at the front.

Therefore, the threatening danger which hung over our Fatherland in the first period of the war was largely due to the faulty methods of directing the nation and the party by Stalin himself. . . .

The main role and the main credit for the victorious ending of the war belongs to our Communist Party, to the armed forces of the Soviet Union, and to the tens of millions of Soviet people raised by the party. (Thunderous and prolonged applause.)

Comrades, let us reach for some other facts. The Soviet Union is justly considered as a model of a multinational state because we have in practice assured the equality and friendship of all nations which live in our great Fatherland.

All the more monstrous are the acts whose initiator was Stalin and which are rude violations of the basic Leninist principles of the nationality policy of the Soviet state. We refer to the mass deportations from their native places of whole nations, together with all Communists and Komsomols without any exception; this deportation action was not dictated by any military considerations. . . .

Not only a Marxist-Leninist but also no man of common sense can grasp how it is possible to make whole nations responsible for inimical activity, including women, children, old people, Communists, and Komsomols, to use mass repression against them, and to expose them to misery and suffering for the hostile acts of individual persons or groups of persons. . . .

Let us also recall the "affair of the doctor-plotters" [publicly "revealed" in early 1953—*ed.*] (Animation in the hall.) Actually there was no "affair" outside of the declaration of the woman doctor Timashuk, who was probably influenced or ordered by someone (after all, she was an unofficial collaborator of the organs of state security) to write Stalin a letter in which she declared that doctors were applying supposedly improper methods of medical treatment.

Such a letter was sufficient for Stalin to reach an immediate conclusion that there are doctor-plotters in the Soviet Union. He issued orders to arrest a group of eminent Soviet medical specialists. He personally issued advice on the conduct of the investigation and the method of interrogation of the arrested persons. He said that the academician [physician] Vinogradov should be put in chains, another one should be beaten. Present at this Congress as a delegate is the former Minister of State Security, Comrade Ignatiev. Stalin told him curtly, "If you do not obtain confessions from the doctors we will shorten you by a head." (Tumult in the hall.)

Stalin personally called the investigative judge, gave him instructions, advised him on which investigative methods should be used; these methods were simple—beat, beat, and, once again, beat.

Shortly after the doctors were arrested, we members of the Politburo received protocols with the doctors' confessions of guilt. After distributing these protocols, Stalin told us, "You are blind like young kittens; what will happen without me? The country will perish because you do not know how to recognize enemies."

The case was so presented that no one could verify the facts on which the investigation was based. There was no possibility of trying to verify facts by contacting those who had made the confessions of guilt.

We felt, however, that the case of the arrested doctors was questionable. We knew some of these people personally because they had once treated us. When we examined this "case" after Stalin's death, we found it to be fabricated from beginning to end.

This ignominious "case" was set up by Stalin; he did not, however, have the time in which to bring it to an end (as he conceived that end), and for this reason the doctors are still alive. Now all have been rehabilitated. . . .

In organizing the various dirty and shameful cases, a very base role was played by the rabid enemy of our party, an agent of a foreign intelligence service—Beria—who had stolen into Stalin's confidence. In what way could this *provacateur* gain such a position in the party and in the state, so as to become the First Deputy Chairman of the Council of Ministers of the Soviet Union and a member of the Politburo of the Central Committee? It has now been established that this villain had climbed up the government ladder over an untold number of corpses. . . .

Beria was unmasked by the Central Committee of the party shortly after Stalin's death. As a result of the particularly detailed legal proceedings, it was established that Beria had committed monstrous crimes and Beria was shot.

The question arises why Beria, who had liquidated tens of thousands of the party and Soviet workers, was not unmasked during Stalin's life. He was not unmasked earlier because he had utilized very skillfully Stalin's weaknesses; feeding him with suspicions, he assisted Stalin in everything and acted with his support. . . .

Some comrades may ask us: Where were the members of the Politburo of the Central Committee? Why did they not assert themselves against the cult of the individual in time? And why is this being done only now?

First of all, we have to consider the fact that the members of the Politburo viewed these matters in a different way at different times. Initially, many of them backed Stalin actively because Stalin was one of the strongest Marxists and his logic, his strength and his will greatly influenced the cadres and party work.

It is known that Stalin, after Lenin's death, especially during the first years, actively fought for Leninism against the enemies of Leninist theory and against those who deviated. Beginning with Leninist theory, the party, with its Central Committee at the head, started on a great scale the work of socialist industrialization of the country, agricultural collectivization and the cultural revolution.

At that time Stalin gained great popularity, sympathy and support. The party had to fight those who attempted to lead the country away from the correct Leninist path; it had to fight Trotskyites, Zonovievites and rightists, and the bourgeois nationalists. This fight was indispensable.

Later, however, Stalin, abusing his power more and more, began to fight eminent party and government leaders and to use terroristic methods against honest Soviet people. . . .

Comrades! We must abolish the cult of the individual decisively, once and for all; we must draw the proper conclusions concerning both ideological-theoretical and practical work. It is necessary for this purpose:

First, in a Bolshevik manner to condemn and to eradicate the cult of the individual as alien to Marxism-Leninism and not consonant with the principles of party leadership and the norms of party life, and to fight inexorably all attempts at bringing back this practice in one form or another.

To return to and actually practice in all our ideological work the most important theses of Marxist-Leninist science about the people as the creator of history and as the creator of all material and spiritual good of humanity, about the decisive role of the Marxist party in the revolutionary fight for the transformation of society, about the victory of communism.

In this connection we will be forced to do much work in order to examine critically from the Marxist-Leninist viewpoint and to correct the widely spread erroneous views connected with the cult of the individual in the sphere of history, philosophy, economy and other sciences, as well as in literature and the fine arts. It is especially necessary that in the immediate future we compile a serious textbook of the history of our party which will be edited in accordance with scientific Marxist objectism, a textbook of the history of Soviet society, a book pertaining to the events of the Civil War and the Great Patriotic War.

Secondly, to continue systematically and consistently the work done by the Central Committee of the party during the last years, a work characterized by minute observation in all party organizations, from the bottom to the top, of the Leninist principles of party leadership, characterized, above all, by the main principle of collective leadership, characterized by the observance of the norms of party life described in the statutes of our party, and, finally, characterized by the wide practice of criticism and self-criticism.

Thirdly, to restore completely the Leninist principles of Soviet socialist democracy, expressed in the Constitution of the Soviet Union, to fight willfulness of individuals abusing their power. The evil caused by acts violating revolutionary socialist legality which have accumulated during a long time as a result of the negative influence of the cult of the individual has to be completely corrected.

Comrades! The 20th Congress of the Communist Party of the Soviet Union has manifested with a new strength the unshakable unity of our party, its cohesiveness around the Central Committee, its resolute will to accomplish the great task of building communism. (Tumultuous applause.)

And the fact that we present in all their ramifications the basic problems of overcoming the cult of the individual which is alien to Marxism-Leninism, as well as the problem of liquidating its burdensome consequences, is an evidence of the great moral and political strength of our party. (Prolonged applause.)

We are absolutely certain that our party, armed with the historical resolutions of the 20th Congress, will lead the Soviet people along the Leninist path to new successes, to new victories. (Tumultuous, prolonged applause.)

Long live the victorious banner of our party—Leninism! (Tumultuous, prolonged applause ending in ovation. All rise.)

ON PEACEFUL COEXISTENCE

While Khrushchev denigrated Stalin's regime as it affected the internal life of the Bolshevik Party, the new dictator continued to adhere to the main lines of Stalin's position in international affairs. On occasion Khrushchev explicitly acknowledged this continuity. After the "secret" speech, for example, he remarked at a reception at the Chinese embassy that all Communists would do well to fight imperialism as Stalin had. And, in the article from which the following selection is drawn, Khrushchev, far from repudiating Stalin's foreign policy, stated that "peaceful coexistence" had been a "basic principle" of Soviet policy ever since 1917, which clearly includes the Stalin era and such remarkably pacific acts as the invasions of Poland and Finland in 1939.

Whatever one thinks of Khrushchev's irenic professions, it is true that the slogan of peaceful coexistence had been used in earlier periods in Soviet foreign policy. Moreover, the same conception underlay the major peace campaign, petitions and all, of the late 1940's, just as Russian Communist power was digging in and attempting to expand in various parts of Europe (cf. Stalin on Churchill's "Iron Curtain" speech of 1946).

On the other hand, the beaming personal diplomacy of Khrushchev, especially in his visits to India and the UN, has attempted to convey through its style the idea that peaceful coexistence under Khrushchev is a new and promising proposal. Perhaps, but only perhaps, this is really the case with respect to one important problem: the awful destructiveness of nuclear war. Stalin did not admit to any special fear of the new explosives, and in 1951 he publicly stated that atomic weapons were no cause for alarm. But we also know that he bent every effort to possess these weapons and that he told the Yugoslav Communist Djilas that he considered them very powerful. In any case it may be said that Khrushchev is far more clearly committed to the view that general nuclear war would be disastrous for all. Short of a holocaust it appears that, as in the days of Stalin, any Communist action is by definition peaceful and any capitalist action is aggressive, even if it pretends to be defensive.

Among the myriad presentations that Khrushchev has made of the conception of peaceful coexistence, the article from which the following is drawn is unique in that it was specially written for and first published in the American quarterly *Foreign Affairs*. This journal is published by the Council on Foreign Relations, a private organization devoted to studies on international affairs. It has many prominent business leaders among its sponsors and is in close touch with policy-makers in Washington. From Khrushchev's point of view the Council probably appears to be an overt office of the "Wall Street clique" that *really* runs America.

In directing himself to such an audience, Khrushchev seems to have felt it desirable to smile less cordially than when addressing, say, Indians, and to pound home in italics the demand that *"everybody should understand the irrevocable fact that the historic process* [of the victory of Communism] *is irreversible."* In short: you capitalists must acknowledge in advance that your surrender is only a matter of time. Then "peaceful coexistence" will be possible.

I have been told that the question of peaceful coexistence of states with different social systems is uppermost today in the minds of many Americans, and not only Americans. The question of coexistence, particularly in our day, interests literally every man and woman on the globe. We all of us well know that tremendous changes have taken place in the world.

Gone indeed are the days when it took weeks to cross the ocean from one continent to the other or when a trip from Europe to America, or from Asia to Africa, seemed a very complicated undertaking. The progress of modern technology has reduced our planet to a rather small place, it has even become, in this sense, quite congested, and if in our daily life it is a matter of considerable importance to establish normal relations with our neighbors in a densely inhabited settlement, this is so much the more necessary in the relations between states, in particular states belonging to different social systems.

You may like your neighbor or dislike him. You are not obliged to be friends with him or visit him. But you live side by side, and what can you do if neither you nor he has any desire to quit the old home and move to another town. All the more so in relations between states. It would be unreasonable to assume that you can make it so hot for your undesirable neighbor that he will decide to move to Mars or Venus. And vice versa, of course.

What then remains to be done? There may be two ways out: either war—and war in the rocket and H-bomb age is fraught with the most dire consequences for all nations—or peaceful coexistence. Whether you like your neighbor or not, nothing can be done about it, you have to find some way of getting on with him, for you both live on one and the same planet. . . .

From its very inception the Soviet state proclaimed peaceful co-existence as the basic principle of its foreign policy. It was no accident that the very first state act of the Soviet power was the decree on peace, the decree on the cessation of the bloody war.

What then is the policy of peaceful coexistence?

In its simplest expression it signifies the repudiation of war as a means of solving controversial issues. However, this does not cover the entire concept of peaceful coexistence. Apart from the commitment of non-aggression, it also presupposes an obligation on the part of all states to desist from violating each other's territorial integrity and sovereignty in any form and under any pretext whatsoever. The principle of peaceful coexistence signifies a renunciation of interference in the internal affairs of other countries with the object of altering their system of government or mode of life or for any other motives. The doctrine of peaceful co-existence also presupposes that political and economic relations between countries are to be based upon complete equality of the parties concerned and on mutual benefit.

It is often said in the West that peaceful coexistence is nothing else than a tactical method of the socialist states. There is not a grain of truth in such allegations.

Our desire for peace and peaceful coexistence is not conditioned by any time-serving or tactical considerations. It springs from the very nature of socialist society in which there are no classes or social groups interested in profiting by war or seizing and enslaving other people's territories. The Soviet Union and the other socialist countries, thanks to their socialist system, have an unlimited home market and for this reason they have no need to pursue an expansionist policy of conquest and an effort to subordinate other countries to their influence.

It is the people who determine the destinies of the socialist states. The socialist states are ruled by the working people themselves, the workers and peasants, the people who themselves create all the material and spiritual values of society. And people of labor cannot want war. For to them war spells grief and tears, death, devastation, and misery. Ordinary people have no need for war.

Contrary to what certain propagandists hostile to us say, the coexistence of states with different social systems does not mean that they will only fence themselves off from one another by a high wall and undertake the mutual obligation not to throw stones over the wall or pour dirt upon each other. No! Peaceful coexistence does not mean merely living side by side in the absence of war but with the constantly remaining threat of its breaking out in the future. *Peaceful coexistence can and should develop into peaceful competition for the purpose of satisfying man's needs in the best possible way.*

We say to the leaders of the capitalist states: let us try out in practice whose system is better, let us compete without war. This is much better than competing in who will produce more arms and who will smash whom. We stand and always will stand for such competition as will help to raise the well-being of the people to a higher level.

The principle of peaceful competition does not at all demand that one or another state abandon the system and ideology adopted by it. It goes without saying that the acceptance of this principle cannot lead to the immediate end of disputes and contradictions which are inevitable between countries adhering to different social systems. But the main thing is ensured: the states which decided to adopt the path of peaceful coexistence repudiate the use of force in any form and agree on a peaceful settlement of possible disputes and conflicts, bearing in mind the mutual interests of the parties concerned. In our age of the H-bomb and atomic techniques this is the main thing of interest to every man. . . .

We Communists believe that the idea of communism will ultimately be victorious throughout the world, just as it has been victorious in our country, in China and in many other states. Many readers of *Foreign Affairs* will probably disagree with us. Perhaps they think that the idea of capitalism will ultimately triumph. It is their right to think so. We may argue, we may disagree with one another. *The main thing is to keep to the positions of ideological struggle, without resorting to arms in order to prove that one is right.* The point is that with military techniques what they are today, there are no inaccessible places in the world. Should a world war break out no country will be able to shut itself off from a crushing blow.

We believe that ultimately that system will be victorious on the globe which will offer the nations greater opportunities for improving their material and spiritual life. It is precisely socialism that creates unprecedentedly great prospects for the inexhaustible creative enthusiasm of the masses, for a genuine flourishing of science and culture, for the realization of man's dream of a happy life, a life without destitute and unemployed people, of a happy childhood and tranquil old age, of the realization of the most audacious and ambitious human projects, of man's right to create in a truly free manner, in the interests of the people.

But when we say that in the competition between the two systems, the capitalist and the socialist, our system will win; this does not mean of course that we shall achieve victory by interfering in the internal affairs of the capitalist countries.

Our confidence in the victory of communism is of a different kind. It is based on a knowledge of the laws governing the development of society. Just as in its time capitalism, as the more progressive system, took the place of feudalism, so will capitalism be inevitably superseded by communism, the more progressive and more equitable social system. We are confident of the victory of the socialist system because it is a more progressive system than the capitalist system. Soviet power has been in existence for only a little more than forty years, and during these years we have gone through two of the worst wars, repulsing the attacks of enemies who attempted to strangle us. Capitalism in the United States has been in existence for more than a century and a half, and the history of the U.S. has developed in such a way that never once have enemies landed on American territory.

Yet the dynamics of the development of the USSR and the U.S.A. are such that the forty-two-year-old land of Soviets is already able to challenge the 150-year-old capitalist state to economic competition, the most far-sighted American leaders admitting that the Soviet Union is fast catching up with the United States and will ultimately outstrip it. Watching the progress of this competition, anyone can judge which is the better system, and we believe that in the long run all the peoples will embark on the path of struggle for the building of socialist society. . . .

The problem of peaceful coexistence between states with different social systems has become particularly pressing in view of the fact that since the Second World War the development of relations between states has entered a new stage, that now we have approached a period in the life of mankind when there is a real chance of excluding war once and for all from the life of society.

The new alignment of international forces which has developed since the Second World War offers ground for the assertion that a new world war is no longer a fatal inevitability, that it can be averted.

First, today not only all the socialist states, but many countries in Asia and Africa which have embarked upon the road of independent national statehood, and many other states outside the aggressive military groupings, are actively fighting for peace.

Secondly, the peace policy enjoys the powerful support of the broad masses of the people all over the world.

Thirdly, the peaceful socialist states are in possession of very potent material means, which cannot but have a deterring effect upon the aggressors.

Prior to the Second World War the USSR was the only socialist country, with only about 17 per cent of the territory, about 3 per cent of the population, and about 10 per cent of the output of the world. At present the socialist countries cover about one-fourth of the territory of the globe, have one-third of the world's population, and their industrial output accounts for about one-third of the total world output.

This is precisely the explanation of the indisputable fact that throughout the past years, hotbeds of war breaking out now in one and now in another part of the globe—in the Near East and in Europe, in the Far East and Southeast Asia—have been extinguished at the very outset.

What does the future hold in store for us?

As a result of the fulfillment and overfulfillment of the present Seven-Year Plan of Economic Development of the USSR as well as of the plans of the other socialist countries of Europe and Asia, the countries of the socialist system will then account for a little more than half of the world output. Their economic power will grow immeasurably, and this will help to an even greater extent to consolidate world peace: the material might and moral influence of the peaceloving states will be so great that any bellicose militarist will have to think ten times before risking going to war. It is the good fortune of mankind that a community of socialist states which are not interested in new war has been set up, because to build socialism and communism the socialist countries need peace. Today the community of socialist countries which has sprung up on the basis of complete equality holds such a position in the development of all branches of economy, science, and culture, as to be able to exert an influence towards preventing the outbreak of new world wars.

Hence we are already in a practical sense near to that stage in the life of humanity when nothing will prevent people from devoting themselves wholly to peaceful labor when war will be wholly excluded from the life of society.

But if we say that there is no fatal inevitability of war at present this by no means signifies that we can rest on our laurels, fold our arms, and bask in the sun, in the hope that an end has been put to wars once and for all. Those in the West who believe that war is to their benefit have not yet abandoned their schemes. They control considerable material forces, as well as military and political levers, and there is no guarantee that some tragic day they will not attempt to set them into motion. That is why it is so much the more necessary to continue an active struggle in order that the policy of peaceful coexistence may triumph throughout the world not in words but in deeds. . . .

We are prepared now as before to do everything we possibly can in order that the relations between the Soviet Union and other countries, and, in particular, the relations between the USSR and the U.S.A., should be built upon the foundation of friendship and that they should fully correspond to the principles of peaceful coexistence. . . .

What then is preventing us from making the principles of peaceful coexistence an unshakable international standard and daily practice in the relations between the West and East?

Of course, different answers may be given to this question. But in order to be frank to the end, we should also say the following: *it is necessary that everybody should understand the irrevocable fact that the historic process is irreversible.* It is impossible to bring back yesterday!

It is high time to understand that the world of the twentieth century is not the world of the nineteenth century, that two diametrically opposed social and economic systems exist in the world today side by side, and that the socialist system, in spite of all the attacks upon it, has grown so strong, has developed into such a force, as to make any return to the past impossible.

Real facts of life in the last ten years have shown convincingly that the policy of "rolling back" communism can only poison the international atmosphere, heighten the tension between states, and work in favor of the "cold war." Neither its inspirers, nor those who conduct it can turn back the course of history and restore capitalism in the socialist countries. . . .

FORTY YEARS OF THE GREAT OCTOBER SOCIALIST REVOLUTION

Four decades after the Bolshevik seizure of power in Russia the Communist regime had much to rejoice over: from a feeble government of a collapsing country it had grown to be one of the two greatest powers in the world and the senior member of a large Communist bloc. But success often brings its own problems and one of the most acute questions of the Khrushchev era has been the peculiar international relations within the Communist bloc. Stalin had been able, except in the Yugoslav fiasco, to cow all European satellites into abject submission while receiving deferential respect from the newly arrived Chinese Communist regime, although the true feelings of this group toward him are hard to know.

It is most unlikely that the international communism of Stalin's last years could have outlived him for long in any case, but Khrushchev certainly invited upheaval with his anti-Stalin campaign, which included the reestablishment of fairly good relations with an unpunished and unrepentant Tito. In the fall of 1956 the armed Hungarian revolt and the shrewder, less heroic Polish demand for more self-government posed a severe crisis that was met only by brutal repression in the Hungarian case and Soviet concessions to the Polish Communists. At the same time the Chinese regime, unhappy over the treatment of Stalin's image, was less complaisant than in previous years.

Hoping to consolidate the Communist bloc, Khrushchev used the October celebrations in Moscow as a pretext for a kind of general council of Communist Parties that held power in their respective countries, the first such meeting since the last Congress of the Comintern in 1935. Out of the deliberations of these leaders came a general declaration of principle. To help prepare the way for this expression of unity, Khrushchev had on November 6 delivered a kind of keynote address to the special anniversary meeting of the Supreme Soviet, from which the following excerpts are drawn. The long address ranged over many subjects, dwelling at great length on the economic and technological development of the USSR; but the most delicate and crucial issue was the one of international Communism. As one unable to impose strict regimentation on all his international partners, yet insistent on conformity in ideology and major policies, Khrushchev attempted an oratorical balancing act of the sort well-known in really competitive electoral campaigns. Yes, the Soviet Union is the senior, most powerful, and most experienced Communist country; but of course it does not dictate to the fraternal parties abroad. Yes, Lenin said each country can find its own path to socialism, but of course Marxism-Leninism sets the general pattern. And there is only one Marxism-Leninism. The new "revisionists" of Marxism are essentially the same type that true Marxists have been combating since the opening of the century.

Even on November 6 Khrushchev's appeal was not quite successful in obtaining voluntary union among the ruling Communist parties. Yugoslavia, the most "revisionist" party present, declined to sign the declaration of the conference and two of those that did sign this formal assent were soon to be even more unruly than Tito's party.

The past 40 years are unprecedented in world history in terms of the saturation of events of the greatest historic importance, in terms of the radical social and economic changes which have taken place in the life of many peoples. They are marked by the triumphal march of the forces of democracy and socialism and the liberation of many countries and peoples from the shackles of colonialism and imperialism. The victory of the October Revolution gave rise to a powerful revolutionary liberation wave that swept the entire world.

International reaction succeeded at that time in extinguishing the fire of revolution in a number of Western countries and delaying for a while the collapse of the colonial system. But reaction was powerless to destroy the seeds sown by the Soviet revolution; nothing was able to halt the victorious advance of the ideas of Great October.

The past 40 years were a period of tempestuous growth, in breadth and depth, of the world Communist and worker's movement. Strong Marxist-Leninist parties came into being, grew and became hardened in the course of the revolutionary struggle; they now unite more than 33,000,000 Communists. . . .

There are now two world systems—the socialist and the capitalist, and each of them has its own specific laws of development.

Lenin teaches that uneven economic and political development is an absolute law of capitalism. Even economic development is impossible under capitalism, with its inevitable anarchy of production, crises and

From "Forty Years of the Great October Socialist Revolution." *The Current Digest of the Soviet Press*, IX, No. 45 (1957). Copyright © 1957 by the Joint Committee on Slavic Studies. Reprinted by permission of *The Current Digest of the Soviet Press*, published at Columbia University. (Originally published in *Pravda*, November 7, 1957.)

bitter competition among monopolies and among capitalist countries. The principle of force is dominant under capitalism. Hence the desire to solve contradictions by means of threats, *diktat,* the unleashing of wars and the seizure of foreign territories, raw material sources and markets. While some capitalist countries are progressing, they are doing so at the price of the pillaging of millions of workers by a handful of capitalist monopolies, at the price of merciless exploitation of dependent and semi-dependent countries. The United States has emerged at the forefront of the imperialist states, and West Germany is now straining to do the same by crowding out and pushing aside Britain, France and other capitalist countries. Such is the law of capitalism—the strong beat the weak, and the naked pursuit of profit holds sway.

Entirely different relations exist among the countries in the world socialist system. Here the law of planned economic development operates. The rapid growth of productive forces and the increase of national wealth characterize the economic development of a socialist society, the goal of which is maximum satisfaction of the constantly growing requirements of the people. All socialist countries, large or small, whether far advanced on the road of socialism or only recently embarking on it, are completely equal. No one of them lays claims to any advantages or privileges. The experience of one socialist country becomes the property of another; the achievements of each country strengthen not only that country but also the entire socialist camp.

The Soviet Union is the first to have built socialism. It has accumulated a wealth of experience and is sharing it with all fraternal countries, helping them to build a new life. In their turn the other socialist countries, which also have great and valuable experience in various spheres of economic and cultural development, willingly share this experience with the Soviet Union and render assistance to the Soviet Union.

The victory of the people's system, fraternal mutual aid and the consistent implementation of the policy of socialist industrialization have enabled many peoples to free themselves from the grip of economic backwardness inherited from capitalism. The tremendous achievements of the socialist countries fill the hearts of the Soviet people and all friends of socialism with joy. Since the formation of the Chinese People's Republic, the volume of industrial production in that country has increased nearly six times. The time is near when people's China, having built a powerful modern industry, will become a mighty industrial power. (*Applause.*) Major achievements in industrial development have been made in Czechoslovakia, Poland, Bulgaria, Hungary, the German Democratic Republic, Rumania, Yugoslavia and Albania. . . .

The Marxist-Leninist Communist and Workers' Parties are the guiding force of the socialist countries. The entire course of development now confronts the revolutionary parties of the working class with the primary task of waging a struggle for greater unity and of expanding the forms of collaboration on the basis of Marxism-Leninism. True to the principles of socialist internationalism, the Communist and Workers' Parties are waging a struggle to consolidate their ranks, a struggle against revisionist tendencies and the harmful prejudices of national exclusiveness and aloofness.

Following their ancient precept of "divide and rule," the imperialists are seizing on any kind of nationalistic prejudice in the struggle against the socialist camp, resorting to ideological subversion under the banner of so-called "national communism." The ideologists of imperialism and their agents are trying to sow the poisonous seeds of chauvinism and bourgeois nationalism in order to set the socialist countries against one another.

Some persons who call themselves Communists and who have swallowed the bait of such propaganda are in favor of socialism but without the dictatorship of the proletariat, without leadership of public life by the working class and its vanguard, the Communist Party, and without implementation of the principles of proletarian internationalism. Our opponents call such a policy "liberal communism," thereby revealing their secret desire to turn Communists into ordinary bourgeois liberals. Where the path of present-day revisionism leads can be seen from the examples of Djilas or Imre Nagy [Yugoslav and Hungarian heretics, respectively—*ed.*], who descended to outright betrayal of the cause of socialism and the basic national interests of their countries. The defeat of the political and ideological positions of these enemies of socialism serves the cause of strengthening Socialism in these countries and the entire Socialist system.

The arsenal of the present-day revisionists also includes praise of bourgeois democracy. This is an old method borrowed by them from the opportunists of the Second International. In their time, the renegade Kautsky, the Mensheviks and the Socialist Revolutionaries conducted a bitter struggle against Lenin and the young Soviet Republic from the same positions. The "wise men" among the leaders of the right-wing Socialists, and along with them the latter-day revisionists, reason more or less as follows: if the Communists were to allow hostile political activity against the socialist system in the countries where they are in power, we would admit that they have freedom and would praise them.

But the revisionists will never have occasion to praise the Communists for such things. We adhere to the Leninist positions of strengthening and developing the socialist state, of developing socialist, not bourgeois democracy, and we will not deviate from Leninist positions! (*Stormy applause.*)

The international experience of building a socialist state in the transition period, especially the lesson of the struggle against the counter-revolutionary uprising in Hungary [in 1956], shows that the working class must know how to defend its power against internal and external enemies and that the working people's state must direct the building of socialism and develop and deepen socialist democracy.

Various forms of the socialist state have arisen under present-day conditions. At the same time it should be stressed that without a Marxist-Leninist Party a socialist state cannot exist, it is impossible to organize the working class as the leading force of society, it is impossible to ensure an indestructible alliance between the working class and the peasantry, and it is impossible to carry out successfully the task of building a socialist society.

V. I. Lenin pointed out that all peoples and all countries would come to socialism, but they would not come to it in the same way. Each country would produce its own variation of the form of democracy, of the form of the dictatorship of the proletariat and, finally, of the pace of socialist changes in various aspects of social life. The 20th Party Congress stressed that the historic experience of the development of all countries that were on the path to socialism fully confirmed this Leninist thesis.

Some people are trying to seize upon Lenin's propositions and the decisions of the 20th Party Congress on the different forms of transition to socialism and of methods of building socialism. They are interpreting these propositions in their own way: if, they say, Lenin put forward and the 20th Congress confirmed and further developed the Leninist idea concerning the various forms and methods of socialist construction, there is no need for unity of the socialist countries. Exponents of this point of view declare that each country can advance toward socialism by its own special way, a way allegedly having nothing in common with other socialist countries.

The theory of scientific socialism takes into consideration and cannot but take into consideration the historical peculiarities of each country which to one degree or another determine the forms and methods of building socialism. This goes without saying. No one who truly stands on revolutionary positions will admit that it is possible, in building socialism, to disregard the socio-economic and historical peculiarities in a country's development. If one proceeds from Marxist-Leninist positions, it is necessary to emphasize not the various peculiarities of each country, but the main, the common element that underlies the struggle for socialism. . . .

The opponents of socialism would like the Communists to start looking for some kind of completely "new," artificial road to socialism for each country, and they would consign to oblivion the great experience of socialist construction which the Soviet Union, China and other countries have. They propose advancing to socialism singly, scattered, so to speak, floundering about separately, moreover on different paths. If this view were adopted, there would probably be so many "paths" that people would lose their way as in a forest and would not know how to reach their great goal. But these calculations are doomed to failure. The Communist and Workers' Parties, having seen through the designs of the enemies of socialism, are giving them a decisive rebuff. They firmly adhere to Marxist-Leninist positions and will not let anyone lead them astray. Attempts to undermine the socialist movement from within and to weaken the socialist countries and parties and turn them against each other are one of the most refined forms of the struggle of imperialism and its agents against the world socialist system. This is one of the chief dangers, and we must conduct the most resolute struggle against it.

The highroad to socialism has already been laid, and the basic forms and methods of socialist construction have been tested by life, by the experience of many socialist countries. It is necessary to perfect these forms and methods, to assimilate and generalize the vast experience accumulated, the experience of the masses' creative work, to enrich it, constantly to develop it in accord with the conditions of each country and each people, to strengthen and not weaken the camp of socialism. Then socialist society will constantly develop and grow, overcoming every obstacle and difficulty.

In their attacks on the socialist countries and their unity, the imperialist circles and their agents are directing their main efforts against the Soviet Union. Why? Because the USSR is the most powerful state. The influence of its example on the international Communist and workers' movement and on the colonial peoples waging a struggle for national and social liberation is great. The imperialists are afraid of the strength and might of the land of Soviets; they fear the ideas of Marxism-Leninism. Hence they are trying by every means to discredit the experience of the Soviet Union and thereby to discredit the great ideas of Marxism-Leninism.

REPORT ON THE PROGRAM OF THE
COMMUNIST PARTY OF THE
SOVIET UNION

In the nineteenth and early twentieth centuries most Social Democratic (Marxist) Parties had placed considerable import on the program of their party, their plan for future action. The Second Congress of the Russian Social Democrats in 1903 adopted a program which occupied a prominent position in party literature before the revolution of 1917. In 1919 a second program, pointing toward the ideal society of the future was introduced, but this document and indeed the whole question of a program slipped into obscurity. In Stalin's day much was made of the constitution of 1936, which summarized the alleged advances to that date but did not attempt to chart the future. Some formal resolutions to write a new program were passed in the Stalin era, but, despite the leader's power to order the delivery of a draft, no results appeared. The nearest approach to a Stalin program for the future society was the brief commentary on the transition to communism in "Economic Problems of Socialism in the USSR" (see pp. 134-137).

For a party that was claimed to be leading mankind to a new, ideal society, this was an anomalous situation. Khrushchev evidently recognized this and saw in the need for a new program a fine opportunity to enhance his rather feeble status as a theoretician of Marxism-Leninism. The Twentieth Party Congress of 1956 had "instructed" the Central Committee to produce a new program and, when the first published draft of the document appeared in 1961, a great surge of publicity and "discussion" followed, reminiscent of the fanfare preceding the adoption of the Stalin Constitution of 1936. Just as the latter campaign culminated in Stalin's speech on the draft constitution, the build-up of the new program reached its zenith with Khrushchev's report to the Twenty-second Party Congress on October 17, 1961. True, the prevailing abomination of the "cult of the individual" did not permit reference to the document as the "Khrushchev Program," but the whole presentation left little doubt that this was the great monument to the wisdom and benevolence of the new leader.

In Khrushchev's commentary on the new program, which was

officially adopted on October 31, 1961, three developments are
especially noteworthy. One is the introduction of a definite time-
schedule of twenty years. For the first time, the party committed
itself to delivery of the ideal society by a particular date. But the
careful reader will find at least two escape clauses: (1) Communism
will be finished "in the main," leaving the possibility that a future
congress may adopt still another program for the "final completion" of communism. (2) Moreover, there is an admission that the
capitalists are able to retard Soviet progress, which suggests that
future delays can be blamed on these "aggressors." A second point
of note is the explicit recognition of the role of the party as the
directing force in the future society; the ambiguity on this point in
Lenin's "State and Revolution" is removed. The state, under that
name, can wither but not the party. Finally, Khrushchev's description of the abundance of the future society, while described in rosy
adjectives, is a warning not to expect too much. As he had previously emphasized in an address to the Twenty-first Congress of
1959, Khrushchev warns that "to each according to his needs" has
its limits—limits that sound rather like those of various non-Com-
munist welfare states.

Comrades, the new program is a new milestone in the history of our
Party and of Soviet society as a whole. Each of our party programs
corresponds to a definite historical stage in the country's development.
Yet all our programs are interlinked. Taken as integral parts of a single
whole, they yield a clear-cut and time-tested Marxist-Leninist theory of
socialist revolution, the construction of socialism and communism.

The programs of the party may be compared to a three-stage rocket.
The first stage wrested our country away from the capitalist world, the
second propelled it to socialism, and the third is to place it in the orbit
of communism. It is a wonderful rocket, comrades! It follows the exact
course charted by the great Lenin and by our revolutionary theory, and
is powered by the greatest of all energies—the energy of the builders of
communism.

What are the main features of the draft program?

The main thing is that it is a concrete, scientifically-motivated program
for the building of communism. The draft shows clearly how the bright
edifice of communism is to be erected. We see how it should be built, how
it looks from within and without, what kind of people will live in it,

and what they will do to make it still more comfortable and attractive. We can proudly tell those who want to know what communism is: "Read Our Party Program."

The draft program marks a new stage in the development of the revolutionary theory of Marx, Engels, and Lenin. The program furnishes an explicit answer to all the basic questions of the theory and practice of the struggle for communism and to the key questions of present-day world development. The Twentieth and Twenty-first Congresses of the CPSU, which introduced much that was new in principle into the solution of the fundamental issues of party life and the life of Soviet society, and into the analysis of the processes of world development, have been of enormous, truly historic importance in the drafting of the program. It would have been much harder for us to work out such a program if there had been no Twentieth and Twenty-first Congresses of the CPSU.

The spirit and content of the draft, in their entirety, reflect the unity and indivisibility of Marxist-Leninist theory and the practice of communist construction. The program defines concrete tasks in industry, agriculture, development of the state, science and culture and Communist education. Comrades, just think of the heights the Soviet people have scaled, if they can chart the perspective of social development for so considerable a historical period.

The third party program is a program of the whole Soviet people. When the party was adopting its first program, it was followed by small groups of politically conscious workers. When it was adopting its second program, it was followed by the working class and the bulk of the working peasantry. Now it is followed by the whole Soviet people. Our people took the party program to their hearts as the greatest purpose of their lives.

The new program signifies a full realization in practice of the party slogan, "Everything for the sake of man, for the benefit of man." It gives priority to matters concerning the further improvement of the people's material welfare and culture, the flowering of the human personality. And that is as it should be. The Bolsheviks hoisted the flag of revolution in order to make the life of the working people joyous and happy. The third party program ushers in a period when all the difficulties and hardships borne by the Soviet people in the name of its great cause will be rewarded a hundredfold.

The draft program proceeds from the new international conditions: Communism is being built not in a capitalist encirclement, but under the conditions created by the existence of a world socialist system, the increasing supremacy of the socialist forces over those of imperialism, of the forces of peace over those of war. The imperialist countries naturally strive to impede the economic and social progress of the Soviet land in every way, forcing it to incur defense expenditures. If this were not so, our rates of development would be still higher. Yet, as the forces of socialism increase and world imperialism grows weaker, more favorable conditions will arise for our economic and cultural development.

Our program is imbued with the spirit of socialist internationalism. Lenin's party has always honorably fulfilled its obligations with respect to its brothers abroad. In October 1917 it lighted the dawn of liberation over the world. It built the lighthouse of socialism that all people can see. That lighthouse illumines their way towards the new social system. Lenin's party will bear aloft the banner of internationalism in the future as well. The party now considers it its prime internationalist duty to build communism in a historically brief period.

The draft program is a document of true communist humanism; it is imbued with the ideas of peace and fraternity among nations. We place the continuously expanding might of our country at the service of peace and mankind's progress. Once the Soviet Union will have become the first industrial power, once the socialist system will have fully become the decisive factor of world development, and once the peace forces the world over will have grown still greater, the scales will tilt once and for all in favor of the forces of peace and the barometer of the international weather will show: "Clear. The menace of world war is gone, never to return." . . .

For the first time, the draft elaborates upon the concrete ways and means of effecting the great Communist slogan, "From each according to his ability, to each according to his needs." It is a proper combination of material labor incentives and increasing distribution through public funds that leads up to the implementation of the principles of Communist equality.

Some people picture living conditions under communism wrongly and narrow-mindedly. They consider just the second part of the formula, "according to needs," and reason something like this: "Under communism you work if you wish, or drift from the Far East to the West, and from the West to the South if you wish; you'll be provided according to needs all the same." A big spoon is all they are equipping themselves with for communism.

We have to disappoint them from the very outset. Their notion has nothing in common with communism. Communist society will have the most advanced technology, the most advanced and best organized production, the most advanced machinery. But it will be people that operate the machines. Machines are dead things unless there is a man to operate them. Thoroughness, good organization and discipline are therefore a golden rule, an obligatory standard of behavior for every workingman. He will not be made to perform his duties by the goad of hunger, as under capitalism; he will perform them consciously and of his own free will.

Everyone will be conscious of the duty to contribute one's labor to the creation of both the material and spiritual blessings. All Soviet people must work so well as to be able to say, when the bright edifice of communism is built: "I have done my bit for it as well."

The classics of Marxism-Leninism emphasized that communism is not fenced off by a wall from socialism, that communism and socialism are two phases of one and the same socio-economic development and the maturity of social relations.

Socialism does not develop on its own foundation. For all its immense achievements of worldwide historic impact, in many respects—the economic, moral—it still bears an imprint of the old system, from which it has emerged. Communism is a higher and more perfect stage of social life, and can develop only after socialism is fully consolidated. Under communism all the survivals of the capitalist system will be completely stamped out.

The fact that communism develops on its own foundation predetermines the distinctive features of its construction. The transition from capitalism to socialism is effected under conditions of class struggle. It involves a radical break-up of social relations, a sweeping social revolution and the establishment of the dictatorship of the proletariat. On the contrary, the transition to communism proceeds in the absence of any exploiting classes, when all members of society—workers, peasants and intellectuals—have a vested interest in the victory of communism and work for it consciously.

It is natural therefore that the building of communism is effected by the most democratic methods, by way of improving and developing social relations, with due account of the disappearance of the old forms of life and the appearance of new forms, of their interconnection and mutual influence. Society will no longer experience the difficulties induced by class struggle within the country. All this will serve to accelerate the rates of social development in the period of transition to communism.

The historical limits of the draft program are twenty years. Why did we set this term? When the draft program was being discussed, some comrades wondered whether the time allocated to the task was not too long. No, comrades. To prepare society for the principles of communism we have to develop the productive forces enormously and create an abundance of material and spiritual values. And that takes a certain amount of time. The bowl of communism is a bowl of abundance that must always be full. Everyone must contribute his bit to it, and everyone must take from it.

It would be a fatal error to decree the introduction of communism before all the necessary conditions for it have matured. If we were to proclaim that we introduce communism when the bowl is still far from full, we would be unable to take from it according to needs. In that case we would only discredit the ideas of communism, disrupt the initiative of the working people and retard the advance to communism. We base ourselves on strictly scientific estimates, which indicate that we shall, in the main, have built a Communist society within 20 years.

What does it mean to build communism in the main? It means that:

—in the economic sphere the material and technical basis of communism will be created, the Soviet Union will surpass the economic level of the most developed capitalist countries and move into first place for production per head of the population, the world's highest living standard will be ensured, and all the preconditions created to attain an abundance of material and cultural values;

—in the sphere of social relations the still existing distinctions between classes will be eliminated; classes will fuse into a classless society of Communist working people; the essential distinctions between town and country, and then between physical and mental labor, will, in the main, be eradicated; there will be greater economic and ideological community among nations; the features of the man of Communist society will develop, harmoniously combining ideological integrity, broad education, moral purity and physical perfection;

—in the political sphere all citizens will participate in the administration of public affairs, and society will prepare itself for the full implementation of the principles of Communist self-government through a most extensive development of socialist democracy. . . .

Comrades, the CPSU is advancing a great task—to achieve in the coming 20 years a living standard higher than that of any capitalist country and to create the necessary conditions for achieving an abundance of material and cultural values.

By the end of the first ten years all sections of Soviet people will enjoy plenty and will be well provided for. Communism will thereby demonstrate its decisive advantages over capitalism in a matter which directly concerns everybody without exception. For the first time in history insufficiency will be fully and finally eliminated. This will be an imposing achievement of the new society. No capitalist country can set itself this task.

There are two basic conditions that will enable the Soviet people to attain the highest living standard. Firstly, a growth of labor productivity, of all social production and of the national income that exceeds the possibilities of capitalism. Secondly, application of the growing productive forces and social wealth in the interests of the entire people. The Communist program of abundance, therefore, rests upon a solid foundation, whereas the numerous bourgeois publicity projects for "public welfare" are no more than new attempts to deceive the masses.

The party considers that while continuing to develop heavy industry and other branches of the national economy, we can and must, in the immediate future, achieve accelerated rates of growth in the standard of living. The real income per head of the population will double in the next ten years, and increase more than 250 per cent in 20 years. The rise in the real incomes of the population will derive from the growth of the national income of the USSR. By 1980 the latter will amount to 720-750 billion rubles, i.e., to approximately five times that of 1960. . . .

Comrades, the grandeur of the new program speaks of the grandeur of our Leninist Party. In giving expression to the lofty ideals of communism our party is creditably performing its mission as leader of the revolutionary transformation of society. Our Marxist-Leninist Party which arose as a party of the working class has become the party of the entire people. In this is manifested the monolithic unity and might of Soviet society, welded by identity of interests and outlook. At all times, in fair weather and foul, in days of triumph and in days of stress, the party is with the people and the people are with the party. The Communist Party is the force that rallies the will, the efforts and energies of our people to accomplishing the tasks that confront us in the new stage of historical development.

Today, when our country possesses vast material potentialities, a highly-developed science and technology, when the initiative of the masses is in full tide, the rates of our progress depend chiefly on the correct implementation of our political line on a countrywide and local scale, on the proper and effective functioning of all our state and public organizations, on their ability to make proper use of the advantage of the socialist system. Hence the need to enhance the directing and organizing role of the party in the period of the full-scale building of communism.

Along what principal lines will the Communist Party develop during this period? We believe that it will be along the lines of:

—further enhancing the role of the party as the highest form of social and political organization, a guiding influence in all spheres of Communist construction; strengthening the unity between the party and the people, extending the variety of forms of party ties with the non-party masses, raising ever broader sections of working people to the level of party members;

—further promoting inner-party democracy, enhancing the significance of the name of party member, stimulating still greater activity and initiative among all Communists, strengthening the unity and solidity of party ranks.

It should be stressed that a new, higher level in the party's political work and organizational leadership has to be attained to correspond to the period of the full-scale building of communism. Adoption of the new program is a great historic act. But it is only the first step. The main thing is to implement the program. The imposing tasks set out in the program place very high demands on the party as a whole, and on every party organization. . . .

At the new stage of our development it is especially important to improve party leadership of the Soviets and the economic, trade union, Komsomol, cooperative and other mass organizations. This is an essential condition for enhancing the organization of the people and for mobilizing their creative powers. While bearing responsibility for the state of work in all spheres of Communist construction, the party organizations must not usurp the functions of government bodies and public organizations. The main thing in the party's leadership of the mass organizations is to mobilize their efforts to build communism; regularly to improve the composition of their leading bodies; to promote, properly place and train cadres.

At the present stage the role and responsibility of the party member are particularly great. The name of Communist is an honored one. Today, as never before, he is expected to be in the van of the struggle for the implementation of the party's policy. In his devoted service to the people, in his social behavior and in his personal life, a Communist should be a model in observing the Communist moral code and thereby contribute to developing and strengthening Communist relations.

A cardinal source of the party's strength and invincibility lies in its unshakable ideological and organizational guarantees against all manifestations of factionalism and group activity incompatible with Leninist party principles.

The measures envisaged in the draft program concerning renewal of cadres, prevention of the cult of the individual, and an extensive promotion of inner-party democracy are truly revolutionary measures. They are organically connected with the party's general plan, its tactics and strategy in the struggle for communism.

Realization of these measures will make it possible to develop on a still broader scale the training of capable cadres devoted to communism, to promote the activity of the party, of all the mass organizations, of the whole people. This means that the development of the economy and culture, the building of communism will proceed still more successfully.

Comrades, the elaboration of the program for the full-scale building of communism is evidence of the tremendous theoretical strength of our party and its Central Committee. Armed with the program, we Soviet Communists feel that we are rising to new heights which give us a clearer view of our Communist future.

What gives us strength? First and foremost, Marxism-Leninism—our ever victorious and constantly developing doctrine. The process of socialist and Communist construction is, at the same time, a process enriching Marxist-Leninist theory through the practical experience of the multimillion masses. The new program is an outstanding theoretical and political document in which are summarized the basic principles of Marxist-Leninist theory on communism and the new conclusions drawn from the experience gained in implementing these principles in socialist and Communist construction.

We are advancing along uncharted paths. We have to elaborate a large variety of problems arising in the course of Communist construction, to develop and define concretely theoretical propositions. Just as the living organism cannot grow normally without sunlight, so Communist construction cannot be accomplished unless its course is illumined by Marxist-Leninist science. The task of our party is to constantly develop our Marxist-Leninist theory, this reliable compass which indicates the way to new victories of communism. . . .

The triumph of communism was always the cherished, ultimate aim of the Leninist Party. This dream of communism is now becoming a reality. Not only our descendants, comrades, but we as well, our generation of Soviet people, shall live under communism! Knowledge of this inspires every Soviet citizen, spurs him on to live and work with unparalleled enthusiasm.

The program shows everyone the place he should occupy in the ranks of the builders of communism, how to work and study, for the good of communism will shine over our land!

The banner of Lenin inspired us in the struggle for the triumph of socialism. And we were victorious!

The banner of Lenin inspires us in the new historic stage of our country's development—the stage of Communist construction!

Under the banner of Marxism-Leninism, under the leadership of the Communist Party, forward to the triumph of communism! (Stormy, prolonged applause, turning into an ovation. All rise. Shouts: "Hurrah!" "Hail to the Communist Party!" "Hail to Leninism!" "Hail to the Leninist Central Committee!" "Hail to Communism!")

CONCLUDING REMARKS AT THE TWENTY-SECOND PARTY CONGRESS

The image of an energetic but tranquil vanguard leading a hearty throng of humanity to Communist society, which was the well-rehearsed theme of the Party Congress of October, 1961, ran into serious competition from quite another image before the meeting adjourned. The congress of a soaring optimism degenerated into a chorus of open or thinly veiled recriminations against its Stalinist past and the defenders of this past.

In the course of the Congress, the explicit revelation of Stalin's cruel treatment of party members was carried forward by various speakers and the decision was taken to take revenge upon Stalin's corpse, which was removed from public display in the Lenin mausoleum to a fairly obscure grave nearby. More important was the verbal revenge taken upon the survivors of Stalin who had defended his name and differed with Khrushchev on various questions of power and policy. The worst offenders, headed by Molotov and Malenkov, had attempted to block Khrushchev at various times, it was said, leading up to an attempt in June, 1957, to remove him from power. The defeat of this "antiparty group" had been announced in July, 1957, but only in 1961 did Khrushchev himself feel able or compelled publicly to dwell on the conflict and to justify his position. Moreover, the list of errant politicians who had not stuck close enough to Khrushchev was broadened by the revelations of the Twenty-second Congress. Most striking was the inclusion of Voroshilov, a close friend of Stalin and long-time senior statesman of Soviet Russia, among the culprits. The humiliation of this old soldier, Politburo member and former President of Soviet Russia was complete several days after the Congress, when he was physically hustled away from the reviewing stand prior to the annual military parade on the anniversary of the revolution.

One reason that the issue of Stalin and his Soviet defenders had to be dragged into the spotlight was the new tension in international communism. Despite Khrushchev's attacks on "revisionism" and his stiff line toward "imperialism" (especially following the U-2 affair in May, 1960), he did not satisfy the largest and smallest mem-

172

bers of the Communist "commonwealth." Albania, quietly but firmly supported by China, attacked the anti-Stalin campaign and Khrushchev's "softness" toward imperialism. Albania did not send observers to the Congress and, after Khrushchev failed to bring round the Chinese representatives, he evidently found it necessary to discourage further disaffection and to show the Chinese that Bolsheviks cannot be pushed around. The following selections from Khrushchev's concluding speech to the Congress on October 27 do convey a sense of stubborn strength, but also illustrate the severity and delicacy of the problem of Stalinism and communist unity.

Comrades! The Central Committee's report and also speeches by delegates to the Congress have referred to the erroneous position of the leaders of the Albanian Party of Labor [equals Communist Party—*ed.*], who have taken the path of combating the line of our party's 20th Congress and undermining the foundations of friendship with the Soviet Union and other socialist countries.

The representatives of the fraternal parties have declared in their speeches that they share our alarm over the state of affairs in the Albanian Party of Labor and roundly condemn the fundamental interests of the Albanian people and the solidarity of the entire socialist commonwealth. The speeches by delegates and by representatives of the fraternal parties are convincing evidence that our party's Central Committee was absolutely correct in reporting to the Congress, openly and as a matter of principle, on the abnormal state of Soviet-Albanian relations.

We were obliged to do this because our repeated attempts to normalize relations with the Albanian Party of Labor have unfortunately borne no fruit. I should like to emphasize that the Central Committee of our party has shown a maximum of patience and has done everything in its power to restore good relations between our parties. . . .

Our great party has more than once been subjected to bitter and filthy attacks from open and covert enemies of communism. But it must be said outright that we do not recall an instance in which anyone shifted with such dizzying speed from protestations and vows of eternal friendship to unbridled anti-Soviet slander as the Albanian leaders have done.

Presumably they expect in this way to lay the groundwork for earning handouts from the imperialists. The imperialists are always willing to pay thirty pieces of silver to those who cause a split in the ranks of the Communists. But pieces of silver have never brought anyone anything but dishonor and shame. (*Applause.*)

From "Concluding Remarks at the Twenty-second Party Congress." *The Current Digest of the Soviet Press,* Vol. XIII, No. 46 (1961). Copyright © 1961 by the Joint Committee on Slavic Studies. Reprinted by permission of *The Current Digest of the Soviet Press,* published at Columbia University. (Originally published in *Pravda,* October 29, 1961.)

Clearly, the Central Committee of our party could not fail to tell the Congress the whole truth about the reprehensible stand taken by the leadership of the Albanian Party of Labor. Our party and the Soviet people should know how the Albanian leaders have been acting. And let the Congress, which is empowered to speak for the whole party, state its attitude to this matter, pronounce its authoritative opinion.

It has been emphasized at our Congress that we are prepared to normalize relations with the Albanian Party of Labor on the basis of Marxist-Leninism principles. How have the Albanian leaders responded to this? They have lashed out at our party and its Central Committee with a blatant, mud-slinging statement.

Comrade Chou En-lai, head of the delegation of the Communist Party of China, voiced concern in his speech over our having openly raised the issue of Albanian-Soviet relations at the Congress. As far as we can see, his statement primarily reflects alarms lest the present state of our relations with the Albanian Party of Labor affect the solidarity of the socialist camp.

We share the anxiety of our Chinese friends and appreciate their concern for the strengthening of unity. If the Chinese comrades wish to apply their efforts to normalizing the Albanian Party of Labor's relations with the fraternal parties, it is doubtful whether there is anyone better able to facilitate accomplishment of this purpose than the Communist Party of China. This would really redound to the benefit of the Albanian Party of Labor and accord with the interests of the entire commonwealth of socialist countries. (*Prolonged applause.*)

It is true, of course, that Communists should so frame their inter-party relations as not to provide the enemy with the slightest opening. But unfortunately the Albanian leaders have grossly flouted this requirement. For a long time now they have been openly attacking the line of the 20th Congress, providing the bourgeois press with food for all sorts of speculation. It is they, the Albanian leaders, who have been shouting from the rooftops about having a position of their own, views of their own that differ from the views of our party and the other fraternal parties. This showed clearly at the Fourth Congress of the Albanian Party of Labor, and has been particularly clear of late.

Why did the Albanian leaders launch a campaign against the decisions of our party's 20th Congress? What treason do they see in them?

Above all, the resolute condemnation of the Stalin cult and its harmful consequences is not to the liking of the Albanian leaders. They are displeased that we should have resolutely denounced the arbitrary rule, the abuse of power from which many innocent people suffered, among them eminent representatives of the old guard who had been with Lenin in building the world's first proletarian state. The Albanian leaders cannot refer without vexation and rancor to the fact that we have put an end for good to the situation where one man at his own pleasure arbitrarily decided all-important questions relating to the life of our party and country. (*Prolonged applause.*)

Stalin is no longer among the living, but we have thought it necessary to denounce the disgraceful methods of leadership that flourished in the setting of the Stalin cult. Our party is doing everything possible to prevent phenomena of this sort from ever again recurring.

One would have supposed that the Leninist line of the 20th Party Congress, which was supported by the fraternal parties, would have met with support from the leadership of the Albanian Party of Labor too, since the cult of the individual is incompatible with Marxism-Leninism. Actually, the Albanian leaders heaped encomiums on the Stalin cult and launched a violent campaign against the decisions of the 20th Party Congress, in an effort to make the socialist countries swerve from this sound course. This, naturally, was no accident. All that was reprehensible in our country in the period of the cult of the individual is manifested in its worst form in the Albanian Party of Labor. It is now an open secret that the Albanian leaders remain in power by resorting to force and arbitrary rule. . . .

People who today advocate friendship with the Soviet Union, with the CPSU, are regarded by the Albanian leaders as enemies.

How is all this to be squared with the vows and protestations of friendly feelings for the CPSU and the Soviet Union that have been heard from Shehu and Hoxha? It is obvious that all their spouting about friendship is nothing but hypocrisy and deception.

This is the atmosphere that prevails in the Albanian Party of Labor, and this is why the Albanian leaders oppose the Leninist line of the 20th Party Congress. After all, to put an end to the cult of the individual would in effect mean that Shehu, Hoxha and others would have to give up their key positions in the party and government. And this they do not want to do. But we are certain the time will come when the Albanian Communists and the Albanian people will have their say, and then the Albanian leaders will have to answer for the harm they have done their country, their people and the cause of socialist construction in Albania. (*Stormy, prolonged applause.*)

Comrades! Our party will continue to combat revisionists of all shades as it has in the past. Steadfastly conforming to the principles of the Declaration and the Statement of the conferences of Marxist-Leninist parties, we have exposed and shall continue unremittingly to expose the revisionism that has found expression in the program of the Yugoslav League of Communists. We shall also constantly combat dogmatism and all other deviations from Marxism-Leninism. (*Applause.*)

Comrades! The 22nd Congress can be called with perfect justice a congress of monolithic unity of the Leninist party and of complete unanimity and solidarity. Our enemies are terrified by the growing unity of our ranks. They are placing hope in the fact that our Congress has devoted considerable attention to discussing the harmful consequences of the cult of the individual, as well as to the definitive exposure of the anti-party factionalist group. But these sterile attempts of the enemies of communism are in vain; they will gain nothing from them.

The difference between the Marxist-Leninist parties and all other political parties is that the Communists, without wavering, boldly expose and eliminate shortcomings and defects in their work. Criticism, even of the sharpest type, helps our forward movement. This is a sign of the strength of the Communist Party, testimony to its inflexible faith in its cause. (*Prolonged applause.*)

Many comrades who have spoken here have angrily condemned the anti-party subversive activity of the handful of factionalists led by Molotov, Kaganovich and Malenkov. Our whole party and the entire people have rejected these schismatics who opposed everything new and who wished to restore the defective methods that reigned under the cult of the individual. They wanted to return to those days, so difficult for our party and our country, when no one was ensured against arbitrariness and repressions. Yes, Molotov and the others wanted precisely that. . . .

The participants in the anti-party factionalist group hoped to seize leadership in the party and the country and to remove the comrades who were exposing the criminal actions committed in the period of the cult of the individual. The anti-party group wanted to place Molotov in the leadership. Then, of course, there would have been no exposure of these abuses of power.

Even after the 20th Congress had condemned the cult of the individual, the anti-party group did all in its power to prevent the exposure from going any further. Molotov said that in large matters there may be bad things and good. He justified the actions that had taken place in the period of the cult of the individual and claimed that such actions are possible and that their repetition in the future is possible. Such was the course of the anti-party factionalist group. This is not a simple aberration. It is a calculated, criminal and adventurist position. They wanted to divert the party and the country from the Leninist path, they wanted to return to the policy and methods of leadership of the period of the cult of the individual. But they miscalculated. The Central Committee, our whole party and the entire Soviet people administered a decisive rebuff to the anti-party group and exposed and smashed the factionalists. (*Stormy, prolonged applause.*) . . .

Here at the Congress much has been said, for instance, about the furious energy displayed by the anti-party factionalists Molotov, Kaganovich, Malenkov and others against the Leninist Party Central Committee and against me personally. Speaking against the course set forth by the 20th Congress, the schismatics concentrated their main fire against Khrushchev, who did not suit them. Why against Khrushchev? Well, because Khrushchev has been promoted by the will of the party to the post of First Secretary to the Central Committee. The factionalists badly miscalculated. The party smashed them both ideologically and organizationally. (*Stormy applause.*)

The Central Committee of our party has displayed an exceptionally high political maturity and a truly Leninist understanding of the situation. It is characteristic that literally not one member or candidate member of the Central Committee and not one member of the Inspection Commission supported the miserable handful of schismatics. (*Prolonged applause.*)

While resolutely pronouncing themselves opposed to all the disgusting phenomena of the cult of the individual, Marxist-Leninists have always recognized and will continue to recognize the authority of leaders.

But it would be incorrect to single out this or that leader, to set him apart from the executive collective or to exalt him inordinately. This is contrary to the principles of Marxism-Leninism. It is known with what impatience Marx, Engels and Lenin spoke out against those who eulogized their contributions. Yet it is difficult to overestimate the great role of the founders of scientific communism Marx, Engels and Lenin and their contributions to the working class and to all mankind. (*Prolonged applause.*)

Feelings of self-praise and any special emphasis on or excessive exaggeration of the role of individual leaders are utterly alien to true Marxist-Leninists. They find it simply insulting when someone tries obtrusively to set them apart, to isolate them from the executive nucleus of comrades. (*Stormy applause.*)

We Communists highly value and support the authority of correct and mature leadership. We must safeguard the authority of the leaders who are recognized by the party and the people. But each leader must also understand the other side of the matter—never to plume himself on his position, to remember that in holding this or that post he is merely fulfilling the will of the party and the will of the people, who may have invested the greatest power in him but never lose control over him. (*Applause.*) The leader who forgets this pays heavily for his mistake. I would add that he will pay while he is alive, or even after his death the people will not forgive him, as has happened with the condemnation of the cult of Stalin. (*Applause.*) A person who forgets that he is obliged to fulfill the will of the party and of the people cannot, properly speaking, be called a true leader; there must be no such "leaders" either in the party or in the state apparatus. (*Applause.*) . . .

FOR FURTHER READING

The companion-volume of the present anthology, *The Bolshevik Tradition: Lenin, Stalin, Khrushchev,* contains an introductory list of primary and secondary books in English which might interest the reader in this field. A much longer bibliography is R. N. Carew Hunt's *Books on Communism: A Bibliography* (New York: The Macmillan Company, 1960).

Many works by Marx and Engels are available in English. Some of the convenient editions are:

Feuer, Lewis S., ed., Marx and Engels, *Basic Writings on Politics and Philosophy* (New York: Anchor Original, 1959).

Freedman, Robert, ed., *Marx on Economics* (New York: Harvest Books, 1961).

Eastman, Max, ed., *Capital, The Communist Manifesto and Other Writings* (New York: Random House, 1932).

Marx and Engels, *Selected Writings* (2 vols., Moscow: Foreign Languages Publishing House, 1951).

Many of Lenin's works have been published in English by International Publishers of New York in the pamphlets of the "Little Lenin Library," *The Collected Works of V. I. Lenin* in eleven volumes, and *Selected Works* in twelve volumes.

The Foreign Languages Publishing House of Moscow has also published many individual titles by Lenin, the anthology, *Selected Works* (2 vols., 4 books, 1950-1952), and is at work on a full translation of his *Complete Works* in forty volumes.

Stalin is represented in various English titles published in pamphlet form, and by these major anthologies: *Problems of Leninism* (Moscow: Foreign Languages Publishing House, 1952); *Marxism and the National Question: Selected Writings and Speeches* (New York: International Publishers Co., Inc., 1952); and *The Great Patriotic War of the Soviet Union* (New York: International Publishers Co., Inc., 1945). His *Works* supposedly includes all his writings from 1901 through January, 1934, in thirteen volumes (Moscow: Foreign Languages Publishing House, 1952-1955). It was to have gone on to cover the later years of his career, but the project was dropped after his death. In fact there are a number of omissions and alterations within the body of material covered in the *Works,* and the collection should be treated with reserve.

Khrushchev is not published in any convenient collection, although the Soviet government has distributed a large number of his speeches, as individual brochures or pamphlets and the anthology *Khrushchev in New York* (New York: Crosscurrents Press, 1961). Another anthology is *For Victory in Peaceful Competition with Capitalism* (New York: E. P. Dutton & Co., 1960). His addresses to the Nineteenth, Twentieth, Twenty-first and Twenty-second Party Congresses are available in the four volumes edited by Leo Gruliow (with Charlotte Saikowski in the case of volume IV) and entitled *Current Soviet Policies,* I, II, III, and IV

(New York: Praeger, 1953; Praeger, 1957; Columbia, 1959; Columbia, 1962) These are drawn from *The Current Digest of the Soviet Press,* the files of which are the best source for Khrushchev in English translation.

There are numerous anthologies or volumes bearing more or less directly or Russian and international Communism, a number of which are noted in the bibliography of *The Bolshevik Tradition.* Of these, the following is especially recommended: Robert V. Daniels, ed., *A Documentary History of Communism,* 2 vols. in one (New York: Random House, 1960). An older anthology of considerable size, covering the period from Marx's lifetime to 1934, is Emile Burns, ed., *A Handbook of Marxism* (New York: Random House, 1935).